The Ox is Slow
but the Earth is Patient

The Ox is Slow but the Earth is Patient

Mick Malthouse
&
David Buttifant

ALLEN&UNWIN

First published in 2011

Copyright © Mick Malthouse and David Buttifant 2011

Allen & Unwin
Sydney, Melbourne, Auckland, London

83 Alexander Street
Crows Nest NSW 2065
Australia
Phone: (61 2) 8425 0100
Fax: (61 2) 9906 2218
Email: info@allenandunwin.com
Web: www.allenandunwin.com

Cataloguing-in-Publication details are available
from the National Library of Australia
www.trove.nla.gov.au

ISBN 978 1 74237 805 3
ISBN 978 1 74237 980 7 (Special Edition)

Internal design by Darian Causby
Set in 11.5/14 pt Bembo by Post Pre-press Group, Australia
Printed and bound in Australia by Griffin Press

10 9 8 7 6 5 4 3 2

The paper in this book is FSC certified.
FSC promotes environmentally responsible,
socially beneficial and economically viable
management of the world's forests.

I would not have been able to write this book had it not been for my wife, Nanette. She has provided me with unwavering love and support since we met at the young age of eighteen. She is my friend, my companion, my advisor, my sounding board and my greatest supporter. Nanette has helped shape who I am today. To her I am eternally grateful.

My children, Christi, Danielle, Cain and Troy, their partners and my grandchildren, Zac, Holly and Lilli, have ridden the rollercoaster of each football season and never complained. Their love and support provides me with strength.

To my friends, players, peers and colleagues and all of the supporters at the clubs I've coached and played for, I would also like to say an enormous thankyou.

The journey continues.

Mick

To Maria—I am so blessed to have you as my wife, friend and mother of our four beautiful children, Nicholas, Emily, Dylan and Bronte. I am indebted to you for your love, unflagging help, patience and support in making this book possible.

My son Nicholas has inspired this book. He has been so influential in defining who I am today. My world is so much richer for him being a part of my journey. I miss him, I love him and I give thanks to have had him in my life.

Part of the proceeds from the sale of this book will go to the N.I.C.K. Foundation: www.nickfoundation.org.au

A special mention to my co-author Mick—it has been a privilege to work with you and I have enjoyed our challenges, triumphs, friendship, laughs and our discussions on life's philosophies.

David

CONTENTS

FOREWORD

A drawn grand final! It had happened only twice before in AFL history. Now wasn't the time for reflection, though. In the late afternoon of 25 September 2010 it was time for Mick Malthouse and David Buttifant to plan.

They walked from the field together, neither victorious nor defeated. Numbness overcame them. A decision had to be made on how to approach the next 24 hours. Hell, how to negotiate the entire week, for that matter. In that moment they knew the challenge ahead would be immense.

The team would first need to recover from this bruising encounter. Then injuries would need to be assessed, player inclusions considered, the training schedule revised, new strategies formed and tactics reworked. This was a Grand Final rematch; they would give it their all. Rarely do you get a second chance.

A week later the two men would embrace on the MCG sidelines, rejoicing in the triumph of an AFL Premiership.

The feeling of relief would exceed joy, though that would come later.

This moment had been years in the making. Like any historic achievement this one was built from a strong foundation. Collingwood's first Premiership in 20 years was celebrated by thousands of ardent supporters and cherished by the people directly involved.

Mick and David had each enjoyed sporting success in times past. This occasion was no less satisfying, though perhaps getting there had been the most difficult. They had to draw on the knowledge and skills gained through those past experiences—both high and low—and through the lessons taught to them by life. Each man is first and foremost a father, with all that that entails. Both men are respected leaders in their chosen professions after years of practice, trial, disappointment and accomplishment. Equally, Mick and David are teachers, with a passion for mentoring and developing the potential of young footballers—for enhancing the lives of the young men in their charge, and of the associates by their side.

Mick became the coach of Collingwood in 2000. The two men teamed up later that year when David was appointed head of conditioning at the club. In the decade that followed they would both be touched by personal tragedy, they would suffer professional hardship and they would claim ultimate success on the football field.

In this book they will each refer to the three P's: persistence, perseverance and patience. They will also write of hope. As the title on the front cover suggests, the ox will succeed if he continues to try, for the Earth waits for him.

Throughout their individual and shared journeys, Mick and David have learnt that sometimes you are the ox and at other times you are the Earth. There are moments when you will be faced with a challenge, and times when you will help another to overcome a hurdle.

In the pages that follow, Mick and David have chronicled the defining moments in their professional and personal lives, the discoveries made in those moments and the lessons learnt. Here they pass them on to you: the leader, the manager, the mentor, the parent and the mate.

With this book, they hope to provide you with insight and inspiration.

Christi Malthouse

INTRODUCTION

THE PARTNERSHIP

'Hey Mick, surely you're not going to have that window open tonight? It's minus ten degrees out there!' David said, looking out at the snow-covered ground in Flagstaff, Arizona.

'Come on Butters, toughen up!' Mick replied as he started on his nightly push-up routine.

David hopped into his bed, knowing full well that later on he would get up, close the window and turn up the heater.

Mick Malthouse, coach of the Collingwood Football Club and David Buttifant, Collingwood's sports science director, have had many a jovial argument about the temperature while rooming together on various football camps. Their relationship began on a purely professional level some ten years back—not long after Mick and his wife, Nanette, and family moved over from Western Australia in 1999 to take up the position at Collingwood. At the end of 2000, David joined the team as head of conditioning. Mick and

David have since shared a lot together, some of which has been life-changing.

Mick began his life in Wendouree in the Victorian country town of Ballarat. Mick's father suffered from a debilitating illness and at a young age Mick took on many of the responsibilities of 'man of the house'. He dabbled with the vagaries of a wild youth, but soon found his niche and began to play football with North Ballarat. He was soon recruited to the then VFL team St Kilda and played 53 senior games for them before moving on to play for Richmond for several years and 121 games, including the 1980 Premiership win over Collingwood.

After retiring from playing in 1983, he started his coaching career at Footscray. Australian Rules football was expanding across Australia and Mick was soon headhunted and appointed senior coach of the newly established West Coast Eagles. Mick led his players to two AFL premierships in his ten-year tenure. His proven success at West Coast influenced the president of the Collingwood Football Club, Eddie McGuire, to recruit Mick as the club's new coach for the 2000 season.

Mick—Leaving West Coast

My move back to Melbourne from Perth was based simply on a family decision. After ten years in the West with the Eagles, it was time. My wife Nanette's mother, Patricia, was in the advanced stages of Alzheimer's disease. Though she was in palliative care, a lot of responsibility was still placed on Nanette's sister's shoulders and for this Nanette felt guilty. My father, Raymond, had ailing health too and was still suffering the effects of Guillain-Barre syndrome. He was also recovering from recent heart bypass surgery. Living so far away from our family was getting more difficult by the year and the pull of home had become too strong to ignore.

Our two eldest children, Christi and Danielle, had completed school and begun their careers, so they stayed in Perth for a while. Our youngest two, Cain and Troy, were just entering the final years of school. We wanted them to complete their education in Melbourne so they also moved with us.

After weighing up several offers from other clubs, I took the Collingwood job. Rock bottom is rock bottom, so the challenges were immense. This whetted my appetite.

Mick arrived at a time when Collingwood was trying to reinvent itself and change was in the air. One of his first decisions was to ask David to join the team.

Mick—On appointing David

On my arrival at the club, one of the deficiencies I noticed in the team was the players' strength and fitness. After 12 months I had no doubt a change was needed in this area—that's when David Buttifant came on board.

I'm a great believer in chemistry between people. Although more than ten years separates David and me in age and our past sporting experiences differ greatly, there was an immediate rapport between us. I was drawn to David's concepts, his lifestyle and what he stood for. I could sense he felt comfortable with me too.

I felt that David's appointment was going to be the right one and it wasn't long before that proved to be true. In a short time he had won total respect from the players. When you can inspire such faith in such a close-knit group as an AFL team, you're a long way along the road to success.

David—Coming to Collingwood

In July 2000, I received a phone call from Dean Laidley, the assistant coach at Collingwood. Dean was a North Melbourne player I'd worked with when I was head of fitness there. It was common to receive phone calls from past players, but this call was not just a friendly catch-up.

I was ready to head back to Melbourne. My time in Sydney with the Olympic athletes had been a wonderful experience professionally, but after a few years in Sydney, I realised my roots were in Melbourne with family and friends. So when Dean called about a job I was all ears. The opportunity was enticing, not just for me but also for my wife, Maria, and our young family.

Around that time other opportunities had emerged from elsewhere in the AFL, including a position with Richmond. Meetings were set up with both Collingwood and Richmond for late July.

The first meeting with two of the Richmond powerbrokers—President Clinton Casey and previous Richmond Premiership coach Tony Jewell—was a lunch at Geppetto's Trattoria in East Melbourne. What an uneventful meeting! It started lethargically and it appeared that there'd been little preparation by either Tony or Clinton. When I ordered a mineral water Tony looked surprised, questioning my abstinence on such an occasion. After the niceties had been covered, Tony asked me how many games I'd played at North Melbourne. I replied that I'd played none and explained that I had spent two seasons at Richmond, where I'd played a couple of games. When Tony asked when that had been, I nearly choked on my mineral water and replied that it was while Tony was coaching in 1986–87. I wondered what sort of workplace Richmond was if this meeting was any indication of how the club operated. No specific roles were defined, nor were any set criteria presented. My unease rose dramatically as each minute crawled by.

Later that afternoon I met with the heads of Collingwood's Football Department—Coach Michael Malthouse and Football Manager Neil Balme. From the very beginning (despite the dank smell of mildew in Mick's office) I felt a sense of belonging. Both of these men clearly had a vision of what they wanted the club to achieve, as well as an understanding of and empathy for the young men in their care. But, most significantly, they emanated a strong sense of family. This latter quality particularly appealed to me.

I recalled something I'd once read about first impressions, and paying attention to the trend of your feelings about the other person over the time spent together. It is a positive sign if you feel increasingly comfortable, and conversely a negative if you feel increasingly uncomfortable.

I rang Maria later that evening and shared the experiences of both meetings. I didn't know what either club was thinking but I knew I wanted to be with Collingwood if an offer came my way. I value hard work, fairness and a passion to win and it seemed clear that Mick and Neil stood for these values too. A few days later Neil rang and offered me the job.

In order to thrive, partnerships need to have a complementary mix of personal chemistry, values, respect, skills and experiences. There are so many examples we can relate to— the builder and the architect, the rod and the reel, Yin and Yang. What is it that makes these partnerships successful? Is it similar traits? Or is it the opposing qualities? Or is it just that they *connect* in a way that often can't be explained?

In the earliest minutes of a meeting you can generally judge your chemistry with someone—just like Mick and David experienced. What you make of first impressions is usually based on a lifetime of experience of interacting with people, but sometimes you know you can trust your gut. Little did Mick and David expect the roller-coaster ride they would experience together at Collingwood in the years that followed. As they began to work closely together to get the best out of the team, a lot of their ideas had to be put on hold due to a lack of funds. Over the past ten years (and with better funding available) they have continued to create strategies and plans, which have contributed to them achieving their dreams—as well as the dreams of those around them. It is all covered in this book.

CHAPTER 1

SHAPING THE TEAM

The vision

The existing culture and traditions of any organisation will influence its vision. Collingwood's unique DNA had organically developed for well over 100 years through some difficult eras, especially the early years of the twentieth century. The club had a particular set of characteristics: hard work, mateship, survival and an ability to go on no matter how tough times were.

But nothing ever stays the same. And for Collingwood, change came in the shape of Mick Malthouse. Mick arrived at the club with what he believed to be a winning formula. He arrived with a vision and set about moulding a new ethos within the club; he and his men took on the task of rebuilding with gusto. Collingwood had only won one Premiership in the past 40 years. Change was not only needed—it was vital.

Going against the grain

Mick's first act at Collingwood was to talk to everyone and try to work out what had been going wrong.

Mick—West Coast transition

One of the most important things in my transition from West Coast to Collingwood was talking to the board members, the staff and the players about why the club was in the position it was in.

Collingwood had unceremoniously claimed the wooden spoon in 1999, finishing sixteenth. This was after finishing fifteenth the previous year and not competing in any finals since 1994. It was in debt and the century-old clubrooms at Victoria Park were in total disrepair.

Most people know how passionate the Collingwood faithful are; couple this passion with immense, stubborn pride and you can imagine how the hierarchies at the Magpies were feeling at this time. Yet there seemed to be no urgency to get to the heart of the problem.

Having come from a very businesslike set-up at the Eagles, where we enjoyed Premiership success in 1992 and 1994 and ten years of consecutive finals appearances, I began to question people within the ranks about why Collingwood had had such little success for so long. I asked what the problems were, who was responsible and what they thought needed to be done to fix the situation.

The range of excuses I received was almost comical. People blamed everything and everyone—from the AFL and the draft system to the umpires, among other things—for the Magpies' unfortunate position.

Perhaps this was the biggest problem of all. You have to admit your weaknesses to truly capitalise on your strengths; if no one at Collingwood was prepared to admit to failures, flaws and limitations, how could they achieve success, strength and achievement?

I felt something needed to be said, so I said it: 'We're the worst side because we're the worst side. We don't do the things required to be the best side. We can't take short cuts and we can't stand still. Other teams have moved past us.'

We couldn't stick our heads in the sand and hide from our problems anymore; we had to face reality if we were ever going to get better and move forward.

Consider some of the game's fallen heroes . . . we've all seen them, former AFL players—some greats of the game—with tarnished images by the end of their careers. They make excuses for their behaviour time and time again. Blaming others, they place the fault with their clubs, alcohol and addictions and so-called 'unavoidable' circumstances, and yet—precisely because they refuse to accept any blame—their difficulties continue.

It's my belief that by standing up and being accountable for one's own decisions and actions, by taking full responsibility for one's own mistakes and misdemeanours, problems can be tackled more effectively, giving the individual (or the team) a chance at redemption.

A lot of changes were made to the Collingwood list at the end of 1999—some of it my doing and some by retirements and other moves. We lost good players who were also good people—like Gavin Brown, who we kept on in a coaching role due to his experience and invaluable knowledge, as well as his strong character. We lost good people who weren't necessarily good players, or quite up to AFL standard. And we lost good players who unfortunately lacked the passion, drive and commitment to continue playing at a high level—the top level.

In 2000 we moved up one position, finishing fifteenth, though this time we did it with more wins and a younger side being developed for the future. In 2001 we finished ninth, just missing out on playing finals.

Early in the 2002 season we had won two and lost three games (having just been beaten by Carlton) when our then CEO, Greg Swann, came to me with some disappointing news. There was a strong drive from within the board suggesting it was my time to go. Some members weren't satisfied with where we were after Round 5 and they wanted a change of coach.

My immediate reaction was anger, then disappointment. Then I asked why. We had a young team undergoing a steady process of development. We were learning and we had been building on a game plan that worked with the strengths of the team. We were moving up. It was time for some self-analysis and a look at how things could be improved.

While angry and disappointed that doubt was undermining the unity I thought we had within the club, realising we weren't all on the same page allowed me to address the board's concerns through the CEO (for the countless time in my career) and I kept my position—for the moment.

When the board voiced its disquiet we started to move forward. This wasn't the first time in my career that my position had been threatened. You're rarely safe as a coach—it just goes with the job—though you do expect to be given every opportunity to prove your worth and you hope that the people in power govern with the same fair and considered business acumen that got them there.

We won the next five games to set up an exciting season and we went on to contest the grand final against an extraordinary opponent. We lost by eight points to a team that would dominate the competition for a further two years. (The Brisbane Lions are recognised as the most successful club of the early 2000s, having reached four consecutive grand finals and won three.) Although I was devastated by the loss, perhaps just as disappointing (when I reflected on the season) was the early knee-jerk reaction of some of the business-focussed board members, who were caught up in the passion of football being results-driven rather than method-driven.

Statistically, an AFL coach lasts five years in the job. I'm pretty lucky to have lasted 28 years! However, I think it's also been achieved through hard work, constant learning, being accountable and ready for change and adapting to stay ahead of the field.

All rational thinking goes out the window when misplaced passion reacts to a complex situation; rash and unwarranted decisions are commonly the result. The supporters can be as passionate as they like— the more passionate the better—but those in charge should remain level-headed. If they see problems, they should raise them and discuss them openly. If

they have ideas, they should relay them to the appropriate person. If they want feedback, they should ask
questions. They shouldn't listen to or give excuses.
They shouldn't remain silent until it's too late. They
shouldn't cast doubt before exploring the reasons.

Today at Collingwood we have a state-of-the-art
training facility, we've had ultimate on-field success
with a Premiership, we've played in more finals than
any other club since 2002 and we are financially
stable. We've overcome many hurdles to get to this
point (both as a club and myself personally). Weaknesses have become strengths, problems have been
addressed, mistakes have been redeemed and success has been achieved.

Rebuilding Collingwood took courage because, in order
to build a new team, you have to remove the old. Mick began
to gather people who had the necessary skills, who shared his
dream and who would creatively contribute in their own right.

During the 2004 and 2005 seasons Collingwood performed poorly. Turbulence was brewing and change was
inevitable. Unfortunately, many who were dedicated and
committed were heavily scrutinised. A review like the Span-
ish Inquisition took place in search of scapegoats.

Intense and dedicated preparation does not automatically
provide immunity to failure; all businesses need to assess and
scrutinise underperformance. The result of such a review at
Collingwood was that several well-respected staff and players
were moved on. Those who were left had to rally together to
develop a stronger and more galvanised unit that had belief
and energy.

Few leaders are prepared to relinquish their own control
to enable others to unleash their creativity. Mick is one of

those few. One of the areas he thought needed attention was the players' fitness. During their first meeting, Mick asked David what he could do for the players. David's response was to ask Mick what type of athlete he wanted him to mould and to promise to do it. From this meeting a mutual respect was born; David knew that he would not coach the team on game day, just as Mick knew he would not control the match fitness of any player.

New methods

Each year, through acceptance of change and embracing innovations, Collingwood continues to develop and improve.

David—Mt Humphreys, Flagstaff, Arizona

An ascent of Mt Humphreys was one of many challenges faced by the players on this training camp. This particular day, 18 November 2009, would be a day of intense physical and psychological challenge among the group. Hiking through the San Francisco Peaks and conquering the summit of Mt Humphreys was no Sunday stroll.

The frenetic pace set by the coach soon challenged everyone's ventilation. It wasn't long before the banter among the group had ceased as each player had to focus on simply breathing.

Among the scattered, white-lined Aspen pines nestling in deep layers of powdered snow, the Collingwood playing squad and support staff trailed up the challenging gradient. The group was confronted by temperatures dropping to 35°C below zero, winds exceeding 100 kilometres per hour and an altitude of almost 4000 metres.

The group's momentum was rhythmic, with no signs of fragmentation or slackening of the pace. We had a mission and a journey to complete. Many had never experienced snow, let alone such reducing oxygen levels as the altitude increased. These young men were being exposed to conditions that displayed little—if anything—in common with their game of football.

Regular assessment of the staff and players' oxygen saturation levels throughout the climb was crucial; if anyone's oxygen levels dropped too low, there was a high risk of acute altitude sickness. As we progressed, some players and staff had significantly reduced oxygen levels. They slowed down their hiking cadence and began falling behind the main group.

With every step the conditions worsened and trepidation magnified. Fear was present, yet not a word was spoken, indicating the true feelings that the group secretly harboured: a desire to abort the expedition and return to camp.

Step by step, the team continued to honour its original commitment. Everyone was feeling pain, yet each was aware of their role as a part of a 'uniform motion'. They knew their quest to achieve the ascent was only achievable as a team. It was a day that the group would be able to draw upon often in times to come.

The discipline of sports science in elite sport has experienced exponential growth over the last 20 years. Before he came to Collingwood, David spent four years working part-time with the North Melbourne Football Club during the mid-1990s under coach Denis Pagan. His studies and research had alerted him to many new training techniques and he was keen to trial them on the Kangaroos.

At one training session in 1995 David placed heart-rate monitors on the players, something not part of his usual training regime. Denis asked what he was doing. When David explained that he wanted to monitor their training intensity and gauge how hard they were working during specific drills, Denis retorted, 'You're going down Scientific Street son!' and told him to take them off as they would distract the players while training.

Like all coaches, Denis was keen for success. He heard that the Adelaide Crows had used heart-rate monitors around the same time and so sports science started to gain his respect. As the club became more determined to win a Premiership, David's position was changed to full-time. By the start of 1996 preseason training, all players were urged to buy heart-rate monitors.

David—Ice baths and Darren Crocker

One of the enjoyable aspects of the job of a sports scientist is to help an athlete get back on track after an injury. In 1995 at North Melbourne I was working with Darren Crocker as he was coming back from an anterior cruciate ligament injury (commonly referred to as a knee reconstruction). Darren—affectionately known as Crock—had been at North for ten years and was well respected. I enjoyed our training sessions together because we were able to inject a sense of humour into our daily routine.

I had been looking at methods to help accelerate his recovery. After one rehab session, I placed six bags of ice in an old bath at our training facilities (under the famous Arden Street grandstand). I told Crock that I wanted him to hop into the ice bath and then immediately jump into a hot bath.

Because we usually joked around so much, he looked at me as if I was fooling around. Straight-faced, I told him that I would get in there first. Realising I wasn't joking, he asked me what this would do for him and where I had got the crazy idea from. I told him that the Russians had been doing it for years and that it had been successful component in many of their training regimes. He laughed and asked where they got the idea. I told him that, in fact, it had come from the Romans some 2000 years ago.

On further questioning I explained that it would decrease swelling and enhance his recovery. As he followed me in he exclaimed, 'You must be mad Butters!' Little did he know at the time that ice baths would become a regular recovery routine in his future years as a coach.

Darren Crocker—Ice baths

As I was lying on the bench at Skinner Reserve after I did my knee, I thought I would have to retire because of my previous injuries. But I was fortunate to play again that year and in '96, '97 and '98.

Because of a number of past injuries, I was apprehensive, but I was also willing to do whatever was offered so I could get back to playing again. I knew we were onto something great and I wanted to be a part of it—you could have told me to walk across hot coals and I would have tried it, I just wanted to get back to my pre-knee-reco form.

Ice baths were very foreign at the time David got me into them. I was doing them before their time as I used to pull up so much better. I was 28 or 29 and I got back in time to play in the preliminary final against Carlton. I continued to use this approach and I remember at the time being about the only one to use ice baths after playing.

After almost four years at North Melbourne, David was given the opportunity to expand his understanding of sports science further when he moved to Sydney to work with athletes preparing for the 2000 Sydney Olympic Games. The innovative techniques used there confirmed many of his theories and he added some highly progressive methods to his repertoire.

Every AFL club strives hard to develop an edge over its competitors and Collingwood is no different. David felt that footballers and their trainers had much to learn from their Olympic colleagues. Why couldn't AFL clubs follow the training formats used by these elite athletes? Wasn't it time to challenge the conservatism of existing practice in the AFL? David believed the time was right to think outside the square if Collingwood was to achieve a competitive advantage. Ice baths had now become a common part of recovery and training in the AFL; another key method he felt was paramount in the success of these Olympic athletes was altitude training.

In 2000, David had spent several weeks in Arizona preparing the Olympic swimmers and he noticed their extremely positive training and performance improvements in that environment. In three weeks these athletes came back with fitness levels that would normally have taken them two months to achieve. He also noticed how they could tolerate greater loads back at sea level and how the risk of overtraining was minimised, giving them the opportunity to focus on quality, not quantity.

Altitude training is nothing new. It has been utilised for the last 30 to 40 years among world-class athletes in a wide range of sports. The challenge for David was to change the traditional thinking of football clubs and convert the sceptics—but change is not easily accepted when training methods are so ingrained.

Although Collingwood had got close in 2002 and 2003, the following years saw substandard performance from the team. David tried to convince others of the benefits of altitude training but met resistance and fear of change.

David put together a presentation for the club president, Eddie McGuire, and well-recognised sporting icon and long-term supporter of Collingwood, John Bertram (captain of *Australia II* in the 1983 America's Cup). They doubted the validity of this method and felt they couldn't justify the cost. David wouldn't back down, however, and continued to provide unequivocal proof of the benefits.

David's tenure at the club was unstable—like that of many others—due to the poor performance of the team. He knew it was imperative that they try something different. Something had to be done to improve the team's position and he believed emphatically that altitude training could be the answer.

One person who did show an interest in learning more about the effects of altitude training was the coach, Mick. He supported the idea and further presented it to the board. Slowly, support for the idea started to grow. As a compromise, David encouraged the players to use the altitude room that had recently been installed at Olympic Park, Collingwood's new training facility.

Guy McKenna—Implementing change

I was assistant coach at the time. The senior coach [Mick] had to implement the idea once he had faith in the fundamentals of the initiative [of altitude training] and how we would make it work.

David continued to lobby and, with the support of Mick, he was eventually granted funding for a trip. The obvious place to go was Flagstaff, Arizona, where he had been with the Olympic athletes five years earlier. In November 2005 the team left for their first altitude training camp.

Altitude training is now strongly supported by the club and has become a regular part of their training regime. More importantly, the players have come to understand its benefits and see it as an effective part of their preparation.

Paul Licuria—Altitude training camp

I know the scientific benefits from altitude are great, but it also gave us an opportunity to develop unity and mateship. It pushes you mentally and physically, but it also gave me the opportunity to help out teammates that were struggling and let them know that they are not alone. It's the guys who don't know how hard they can push that you can help push through.

Mick—My defensive style

It's fairly well recognised that I have always coached with a defensive style and strategy. I have found this relatively easy. My playing days began in country Victoria and then I moved into the VFL scene under Allan Jeans at St Kilda. In my 121 games with Richmond I was played in a defensive position, which I thoroughly enjoyed, and I eventually took on a leadership role in this area. Defence came naturally to me.

To support the defensive mechanisms in my coaching I was buoyed by history. Historical evidence shows that in most ball sports, the best defensive side has the greater chance of victory in the big games that count (like finals).

In the past, when a team under my reign hasn't quite matched it with the powerhouses of the competition, debate has always followed that we were too defensive and never attacked enough 'through the corridor'.

I am totally bemused when I review video footage of our games each week and the same commentators (some of whom are former coaches) incessantly drive the subject to death—'Why don't they use the corridor?' One critic in particular—Malcolm Blight— had great success as a player and coach (with Geelong and Adelaide). He played and coached his own way to achieve that. Surely he can realise that each team has its idiosyncrasies and each coach needs to support those idiosyncrasies.

This media-driven criticism came to a head in 2009, when Collingwood was seen to be a great boundary-driven side. What saved us from total ridicule, however, was the fact the great St Kilda side (which won 20 home-and-away games and contested the grand final) had the same ratio of boundary play as Collingwood. Criticisms of our defensive structure became subdued by the end of the season as the Saints' similar style was praised.

I am still amazed that the critics never took into consideration a key point from other ball sports—when in doubt, attack from the widest part of the ground:

- In soccer, you cross to the extremities to bring the ball back across the goal mouth. When under pressure, the ball is kicked out of bounds. Yes, it lands in the hands of the opposition, but it allows for the chance to take a breather and regroup.
- In rugby union, you kick for territory and to see it across the line. Again, this enables the team a short period to readjust.
- Rugby league is no different.

The bottom line is that if you make a mistake, make it wide, not through the corridor (where you can be punished more rapidly and severely.)

In 2010, our Premiership year, our percentage of boundary-line play was as high as in 2009 and yet it drew very little criticism. There were passing comments that Collingwood always went to the boundary first before getting the ball into the scoring zone, but as we were the second-highest scoring team for the season, it couldn't be seen as a negative and ridiculed anymore.

Had we listened to the earlier criticism and changed to please our critics, or panicked and tinkered with our methodology, we would have become victims of fright. We could have followed the great and successful Geelong side (2007–2009), which was highly corridor-conscious—but who knows if we would have won a Premiership with that method? I highly doubt it.

We stuck rigidly to what we believed would

create the best result for our team and we won a Premiership.

A team will respond to the strategies and game plan of its coach. However, a team will only embrace a plan its members truly believe in. Fortunately, our team embraced the plan. Our goal of being one of the top four defensive teams of the competition was achieved and success followed.

We continued with what we believed was the best-case scenario for our team against massive scrutiny. And it paid off. This was a lesson learnt.

It does take courage. Results won't always work for you and when they don't, you have to accept that you'll be severely questioned. But it's important to always be true to yourself and true to your team. You'll eventually get the result you are after. Coaches and leaders aren't hired and fired on looking pretty; it's the results that count.

As an interesting side-note, it's quite remarkable that after all of the debate, the 2010 grand finals were played out between the two best defensive sides of the competition. The draw and the replay still allowed for scoring (Collingwood kicked 16 goals and St Kilda 7 goals in the replay) and therefore an exhausting, entertaining and fantastic game, but it was defence that won out in the end.

It's important to recognise that change is inevitable if you want to achieve and sustain a competitive advantage. When you're the instigator of change you need to be prepared for resistance. And if you fail, be prepared for criticism. But if you follow your convictions honestly, this criticism is much easier to bear. And who knows . . . you may get it right!

This pertains to life in general, not just sports. People and the world around us constantly evolve. Obstacles and set-backs will continue to come, as will the sceptics. It's keeping the belief strong and being prepared to revise your approach to deal with reality that is crucial.

CHAPTER 2

BAKING A GREAT CAKE

Every cake uses basic ingredients, such as eggs, flour and sugar. An edible, tasty cake can be created with these and a couple of other essential ingredients. The decorations are where one cake can vary from another. A basic cake, with the help of fresh ingredients, icing sugar, lollies and edible decorations, can be made into a prize-winning masterpiece.

Similarities can be found with a football team. All teams require the basic necessities—sound football skills, above-average fitness levels and set game structures. After it acquires these essential foundations, extra, finer details can be added—like an advanced medical team, state-of-the-art training facilities, proficient and committed coaches who keep abreast of game changes and more. The *piece de resistance* is determined by formulating—with precision—the finer details. Just as a cake can evolve from a basic sponge to a colourful, artistic, delectable dessert, a football team can go from being average to an exceptional Premiership side.

When Mick arrived at the Collingwood Football Club, he had a basic cake. As he worked with the team over time, the recipe continued to evolve. This was achieved with inputs such as advanced training resources, specialised staff in key areas and continued recruitment of highly skilled players with character. Then he added some more ingredients— ongoing strategic planning, reviewing, construction, belief and vision. The plan was set, the ingredients were fresh and high-quality, and the method was gradually refined to create a prize-winning cake.

The plan

Few goals are ever successfully achieved in life without some type of plan to follow along the way. Rarely will an ad hoc method take you to your desired destination. Sure, some people or teams have landed on their feet unexpectedly or by a stroke of luck. But luck is not enough to create a successful team. Sure, a stroke of luck can enhance a plan; it's never knocked back, but it must not be mistaken for the way to success.

Think back to the Winter Olympic Games in 2002 at Salt Lake City. In the short-track speed-skating event, the Australian skater Steven Bradbury was coming last. One of the skaters slipped and caused the rest of the pack to fall over. This fall enabled Steven to glide on past the fallen skaters and claim the first Australian Winter Olympics gold medal. Even Stephen, who got lucky in the final race, would have had goals to achieve as well as a strict training program. The fall by the other skaters was his stroke of luck and he took hold of that opportunity to win gold.

In order to be successful, a sportsperson or a team must have a goal and a plan and this plan must be specific to the desired outcome. An Olympic swimmer, for example, would work with a four-year plan, while a first-year AFL rookie doesn't have the luxury of this length of time and may only have 12 months to achieve his plan. For an AFL team, winning a Premiership takes patience and time, but—most importantly—it requires a plan. Make no mistake—just as a great cake requires a great recipe, a team aiming to win a grand final must have a great plan!

Trevor Nisbett (CEO, West Coast Eagles)— Mick's first day

On his first day, Mick wanted to go through the team to see who he had. He then requested the videotapes of the previous season to view the opposition. We didn't have any to provide. We had never done this before. Mick placed a strong emphasis on the opposition—that was the start of Mick's impact and planning at the club. This was the key to changing the culture.

When Mick arrived at Collingwood his aim was to rebuild. While this was happening—somewhat unexpectedly—Collingwood played in the 2002 and 2003 grand finals. But after losing both games, the desire to win a Premiership strengthened and involved even more rebuilding. It commenced, with fortitude, in 2004 with a new plan. The difference from these previous years was that all players and coaches strongly believed and were committed to this plan.

The journey of success was a six-year one and it required a strategy with strong core principles that were adhered to. But having a plan is not just about principles.

A plan directs a team's efforts towards goal-relevant activities and away from goal-irrelevant actions. When someone is given a target to strive for it can lead to greater effort. At Collingwood, individuals have become more likely to work through setbacks if they are focussed on a plan and working towards a goal.

Even in times of doubt, the plan was constantly referred to as a reminder of what the club was aiming for. This required them to revisit their reasons for designing the plan as they did. At times there was debate and conjecture—it's especially in times of failure or doubt that plans come under scrutiny. In a publicised competition like the AFL, this scrutiny often comes from the media and the public. It's important not to be influenced by outside comments or to allow knee-jerk reactions. Plans must be adhered to for a decent period of time and be given a chance to work.

Nathan Buckley—Planning
You need to make incremental changes and then you start to evolve. I wasn't afraid to change.

At Collingwood's planning sessions, outcomes are identified and measurable goals are set. After identifying the team's aims and goals, they are prioritised and broken down into smaller and larger goals. The smaller ones must be progressive and achievable; they need to be followed regularly—such as daily. Meanwhile, it's essential to keep the larger goals in mind too. The bigger picture must always be there and it should be referred to often. A player's smaller goals for a season might be to improve his speed and to win a two-kilometre trial, while his bigger goal might be to make the finals.

David—Phillip Island Leadership Camp, 2003

Mick and I had organised a leadership camp for late January 2003. Our plan was to challenge our leaders, create unity and establish an environment where they could develop their resilience and enhance their leadership skills. This was to be done by circumnavigating Phillip Island by means of sea kayaks, paddling surfboards, running and cycling. Chris Dallinger, a trained recreational leader, was added to the team.

Although Chris has vast experience in each of these legs—as well as sound knowledge of the island's terrain and waters—he had never before led a group in a complete and uninterrupted circumnavigation of the whole island. Meanwhile, Mick's queries about the weather patterns, tides and wind patterns (due to his passion for meteorology) was lost on us all—one would have thought he majored in atmospheric physics with all the questions he was asking. I chuckled to myself at his passion for the environment and imagined him doing the weather on the news.

The night before the challenge, the players were briefed. Emergency procedures were established, leaders of smaller activities or groups were appointed and an outline of the plan and its purpose was delivered. We estimated that the circumnavigation would take under seven hours. We identified key landmarks where the party would rest, rehydrate and refuel.

The group was led convincingly by the captain, Nathan Buckley. He executed most legs with strength, courage and perseverance. His leadership group battled on, following his example. But everyone has their weaknesses; in Nathan's case it was the surfboard paddle leg. Although accomplished at many aspects of sport, paddling was not his forte. Trepidation was also in the air after the group had seen a seal washed up on the beach with a big shark's bite out of its torso.

Although we conducted this event in summer and hot weather is to be expected, on the day we were faced with a scorcher: a 37^{0}C day. By the paddling stage the group was halfway through the circumnavigation and running behind our estimated schedule. The heat was increasing as the main group waited on the beach for 20 minutes or more for Nathan and Mick. With the heat beating down, getting hotter by the minute, the group waiting on the beach for Nathan and Mick were getting frustrated and anxious to finish, knowing they still had half the course to complete.

Everyone has their breaking point. Nathan snapped, 'This event is crap!' in response to the ribbing and complaints from the group. Jimmy Clement and Scott Burns couldn't help themselves fuelling the fire with banter about Nathan's incompetent paddling. Mick, on the other hand, had a smirk on his face, as though he had just successfully conquered one of his great fears. I'm not sure how much surfing (and shark) experience he had had back in Ballarat!

We had anticipated that the final leg would be completed during low tide. But because of the difficulty of the heat and unknown terrain and conditions for the competitors, we were way behind schedule.

This led to another obstacle: the tide! The last leg was a bike ride along the beach, but the incoming tide meant that there was no firm sand to ride on and the party were forced to walk and carry their bikes.

By this stage they were exhausted and the heat had taken its toll. They resorted to schoolboy antics, cursing and swearing at each other and threatening me. I had to walk 20–30 metres in front of them to avoid listening to their abuse; my own exhaustion was testing my patience and I couldn't guarantee that I wasn't going to curse back at them.

Eventually, we got back on the bitumen and were able to ride back to camp, in spite of Anthony Rocca having a puncture on the way. In that time, Nathan showed true leadership and encouraged the party to keep pushing on, which regrouped them. I knew that although it had taken us much longer than anticipated to achieve our goal, we had seen our true leaders come to the fore and reveal their weaknesses, as well as their ability to survive under such extremities, and return to their positions of leadership. Our plan had worked and our goal was achieved, despite it taking almost 12 hours to complete.

Nathan Buckley—Circumnavigating Phillip Island

If the challenge was 99 kilometres around the island, I reckon I enjoyed 98 kilometres of it. I felt fit going into the event; I recall never taking myself out of the moment and I really embraced the challenge and the working together. I had a sense of accomplishment and sharing this with the group was great, which is why I am so glad I played a team sport and not an individual one.

As a leader, I made it a race and I was hoping the others did as well. In a challenge like this, leading by example is one thing, but there is no point if there is no one following. It took me a while to work that out. It's not how hard you do things; it's about helping others out.

Ingredients

For a plan to be initiated, you need to gather the necessary ingredients. A cake won't be tasty if it doesn't have good-quality ingredients and a football team won't be successful if it doesn't have well-conditioned and skilled athletes. An AFL team aiming for success requires components including players, staff, coaches, equipment, technology and resources. But it's not just a case of gathering these ingredients; it's also necessary to know how get the most out of them. You need to get to know the athletes on an individual level and understand their abilities, limitations and potential. Those working with the athletes must also know themselves on this level. They must be familiar with the methods they will be undertaking and know their own limitations in following them.

Knowledge is essential in understanding the other ingredients as well. Resources and equipment must be fully understood—it's pointless having state-of-the-art equipment and not knowing how to use it beyond the basic functions (or having staff who don't know how to use it). Some flexibility is also required here; resources can be updated regularly and it's important to keep abreast of new systems and developments.

A sound sports-science medical team was a crucial ingredient in Collingwood's plan. This comprises doctors and physiotherapists who are specialists in sports medicine with extensive experience working with elite athletes. Assisting the sports-science medical team, you need strength and conditioning staff, sports-science staff, dieticians, masseurs and trainers. Complementing this are volunteers who have an understanding of the operations of the team and the club—usually the loyal foot soldiers who do the grunt-work for the love of the club. Each of these groups plays an integral role as part of the team. Each member of a team needs to know their role and play their role well; if there is confusion and uncertainty, doubts can arise.

David—The drawn grand final: Remaining positive

Geoff Walsh (Director of Football Operations) and I caught up on the Sunday morning following the 2010 drawn grand final to discuss operations for the week. I mentioned to Walshy that it might be helpful if he addressed the staff on the topic of remaining positive. This included part-time staff, trainers and volunteers. Walshy has a respected but firm approach and he doesn't mince his words. I knew he could deliver this message clearly and concisely.

Before the players went out for their recovery session, Walshy gathered the staff in the lounge area. The group was mentally flat—as we all were—from the previous day. They had been discussing how disappointing it was that we didn't win and how they were not looking forward to going through it all again. They were understandably emotionally drained. They appeared anxious as it was unusual for the director to call them all in at once, but the drawn grand final was an unusual situation.

Walshy began by acknowledging their efforts and commending them on how they conducted themselves. He made mention of how we were all disappointed, but emphasised that no one was more disappointed than the players themselves. The gist of the message was to remain positive no matter how low they were feeling. He demanded when they were in the company of the playing group that it was important to keep positive. Any negative talk could destabilise the group. He reminded everyone to know their role and play their role—let the baker bake the bread! Although flat, everyone acknowledged this and knew they had a duty to perform and promised to do it.

The players are the vital ingredients and each player displays his own individual characteristics, inside and out. Vast differences among players are common—for example, Jarryd Blair, a midfielder, is only 174 centimetres tall and weighs 75 kilograms, compared to our ruckman, Darren Jolly, who stands at 203 centimetres and weighs 107 kilograms. These players' physical profiles show how completely different two members of a team can be, yet both contribute vitally to the mix.

In team sports, everyone is an important part of the mixture and each 'ingredient' needs to be nurtured to maximise the 'flavour'. Take the young rookie player who is lacking AFL-level strength and power in his first year of football. It takes time to develop a player to his maximum potential. However, although not at his peak, this rookie can offer youthful energy that older bodies can't. The important thing is to be aware of what you've got and what part each element has to play.

Mick—Marty Clarke

Eighteen-year-old Marty Clarke came to Australia from Ireland, where he was already a star in Gaelic football's MacRory Cup and with the Gaelic Athletic Association club An Riocht. He displayed an extraordinary ability to use the ball. His strengths were kicking, stamina and courage.

He was an instant hit with the Magpie Army for all of these qualities and, in particular, his Gaelic football skill of toe-poking the ball off the ground into his hands on the run. However, as time went on, his deficiencies were also exposed.

I am a great believer in working on your strengths *before* your deficiencies to gain confidence rather than lose it. But you do have to acknowledge your weaknesses so you can address them in time. What became obvious to me with Marty—and I knew other coaches would soon pick up on it too—was his lack of a 'right side', his struggle with handpassing and his inability to effectively negotiate stoppages, which, in turn, exposed our backline.

Perhaps what worried me more was what he said to me after a game against Sydney in June 2009. It was a typical match between Collingwood and the Swans, with only three points separating us at three-quarter time. We had lost Scott Pendlebury early and looked out on our feet at the final break. We managed to generate enough of the footy in the last term, though, to provide Alan Didak and Leon

Davis with the opportunity to score—they finished with five goals between them—so we had the game stitched up by the 18-minute mark and eventually won by 23 points.

In the rooms after the game, Marty told me he wanted to play forward or in the midfield rather than continue in the backline. When I asked him why, he said, 'I want to win games off my own boot, like Dids and Leon.' I then started to doubt his acceptance of the role he had to play within our structure and his willingness to be a team player.

Please note that Marty is a fantastic kid whose company I enjoyed off the field. It was his ill-directed ambition on-field that troubled me. He played a very important role in the Magpie backline. His debut against Sydney in 1997 was dubbed by some of the media as one of the best debuts in the history of the game. His ability to gather a high number of possessions made him dangerous to the opposition. But with the public applause for stopping a goal not as evident as for kicking one, Marty was wanting more personal accolades.

At home in County Down, Marty was a superstar and did kick winning goals, which the supporters loved. He was admired and his skills coveted. As a small fish in a big bowl in the AFL, however, his praise was limited and he missed it.

When I realised he wasn't taking responsibility for his role in our team structure, my faith in him faltered. It was his own desire to return home to the spotlight, though, that influenced his decision to retire from the AFL at the end of that season, leaving many of us wondering, 'What if?'

Marty may make a comeback to the AFL one day and I hope he does. I hope he learnt from his encounters and contests in his three years with Collingwood. Not everyone can be a superstar, but we can fulfil our roles within a team to the best of our ability—for most, that's enough.

Blending

Australian Rules football is a unique game that incorporates many characteristics because it's a hybrid game. The athlete needs to have strength, power, agility, endurance, skill and tactical perceptiveness. The key is to stimulate and develop each characteristic without doing too much in one direction. The physical capabilities of a player are a crucial ingredient, but there are so many other facets. Performance is optimised by integrating these physical characteristics—the tactical (game plan) and technical (skills)—into one program.

Bringing all the key ingredients into a program takes careful planning. You need to identify what changes you can make without compromising other areas of performance. If, for example, your team's tackling had been poor throughout games, it would seem obvious to spend more time working on this in their physical training. But on the flip side, this can induce or provoke injuries, which can exacerbate the problem.

The action plan must consider all the necessary ingredients so that a process can be established to ensure a balanced approach. Three factors need to be considered: volume, intensity and frequency. Volume means the overall time spent; intensity refers to how hard the athlete works; and frequency indicates the amount of repetitions in the activity.

The difficulty of programming with team sports—particularly Australian Rules Football—is that there are conglomerations of areas that need to be stimulated and blended effectively and precisely. When there's an imbalance—too much emphasis on endurance training to the detriment of strength and power training, for example—overall performance commonly suffers. This could occur when an athlete trains for five days doing ten-kilometre runs each session and one weight training session a week. If this pattern is reversed, of course you would see the opposite effect. The blend must be precise so that performance is enhanced and progressions can be achieved at the right level. With careful planning and regular reviews, responses can be monitored so that the plan can evolve.

Sampling

In cake-making things are not always successful; a sponge cake may not rise up to be light and fluffy but may instead end up looking like a pancake. When trying to make a successful sponge, the typical response would be to go back and review your ingredients, method and timing. Assessing the performance of a team is no different. When, for example, a team's stoppage structures are not working at centre bounces, a review of the plan and the execution is necessary.

The simplest way to assess whether a cake is successful or not is to taste it. Similarly, the simplest way to assess a football team is to look at the game results. The ultimate assessment of a game is the scoreboard itself. For a more detailed assessment and closer analysis of a team (or a failed cake), a scientific approach is used. In analysing a failed cake, you might ask: Was the oven temperature correct? Were the ingredients measured correctly? Were they blended in the right order, for long enough and at the correct speed? From this review process a cause-and-effect response can be determined and then the procedure can be adjusted until the outcome is perfected. Reliable testing procedures are put into place that will enable programs to be assessed accurately.

> *Virtually every company will be going out and empowering their workers with a certain set of tools, and the big difference in how much value is received from that will be how much their company steps back and really thinks through their business processes on how their business can change, how their project management, their customer feedback, their planning cycles can be quite different than they ever were before.*
>
> Bill Gates

In every training session and after every game some form of assessment is conducted to ensure that key performance indicators (KPIs) are met. These could from range from game statistics or blood markers of fatigue to physiological performance testing in the gym. From this monitoring process valuable feedback is obtained, which can be prescriptively applied to the program. What often occurs in times of poor performance is that opinions interfere with evidence-based research. The problem is that these ingrained opinions can masquerade as fact, but it is in validated and accurate evidence that the answers lie.

Each year at the end of the season the football department, facilitated by Geoff Walsh, conducts a review of the preseason and the full football season. This incorporates a comprehensive evaluation of the technical, tactical and physiological aspects of performance and preparation. It's an opportunity to review all areas comprehensively and assess whether the KPIs were met. Furthermore, healthy discussion and debate takes place at this time and new interventions are proposed. The athletes and the program designers are accountable and the results of the review force people to evolve, renew and rejuvenate their models.

These types of assessments can instil confidence in what is being implemented. There will continue to be conjecture presented by the so-called experts in the media, supporters and the general public about their team's performance. Once confidence in the processes has been established, external comments or theories become inconsequential. The key people driving the program—as well as the drivers in the program—are the only critics who can improve the processes.

> *If my critics saw me walking over the Thames they would say it was because I couldn't swim.*
>
> Margaret Thatcher

Adding the icing

The difference between a prize-winning cake and a basic cake can very often lie in the added extras. A plain cake can be transformed into a visual masterpiece with icing and other decorations. So where are the similarities with a football team? What sort of icing can be added to make a team a Premiership side?

As outlined earlier, all teams should have a plan. But how do you know if the plan is a good one? Is it detailed and specific to each individual's needs or is it a generic one for the whole team, regardless of ability level, age and injury? Has it been prepared with sound systems as its basis? Is it the latest fad or the best procedure? Are the ingredients the best available?

Although a team may only be participating at a local level, it can still scrutinise its procedures by using reliable, proven methods. Its leaders can keep an open mind and look outside the box to see if their procedures complement the program.

Local teams can encourage the use of player diaries, ice baths, good eating and sleeping patterns and a balanced lifestyle. They can seek competent masseurs and other external resources to assist with athletes' recovery. They can encourage the use of appropriate and validated supplements.

So what is the cherry on the top? Over recent years, Collingwood has developed its training methods to include all of these things. They have ensured that they have the best professionals on hand. They have not only used these methods but also regularly reviewed, analysed and reviewed again. They have monitored mood and energy levels, developed methods in their sports psychology to really know their players and conducted open conversations without being judgemental.

Collingwood has pursued new ideas and scientific procedures that—although sound and proven in other sports—have not yet been trialled in the AFL. In addition to altitude training, meditation, for example, is now conducted with the team and used to collectively enhance its power. In essence, success is no accident—you must set goals and implement them with diligence.

But this formula is not just related to sport and baking cakes. These strategies can be utilised in many areas of life—they can be applied to your career, study, business, leisure and hobbies and even the daily routine of life.

David—The small changes that can make a difference

At the beginning of the preseason in 2005, we gathered the playing group in the theatrette for a brief education session. I asked the question, 'How many of you recall the Sydney Olympics back in 2000?' The majority of hands went up. I followed up that question by asking the group who could remember the 10,000-metre race. Only about half raised their hands, most apprehensively. Then I asked, 'Well, have you heard of the great Ethiopian runner Haile Gebrselassie?' The boys nodded and I had their attention.

It was impressive, I explained, that he was defending the Olympic 10,000-metre gold medal. But what was even more remarkable was the narrow victory by Gebrselassie over the Kenyan Paul Tergat. Tergat ran a sub-27-second for his last 200 metres. Gebrselassie went one step further and ran the last 200 metres in under 26 seconds! I asked them if they could imagine running under 26 seconds for the last 200 metres after having run 24 laps at well under three-minute-a-kilometre pace. As you can imagine, the runners were going for it hammer and tongs! But what I found so striking was that the difference between winning and losing was only 0.09 seconds for an event that lasted over 27 minutes.

This margin in the great 10,000-metre event, I explained, was smaller than the difference in the final of the 100-metre men's sprint. The difference between winning the ultimate prize—the Olympic Gold medal—and coming second was less than half a per cent.

When a game of football ends with one team winning by a margin of a point—or even in a draw—it's no different. It's just like these two great athletes who competed in this famous race.

I suggested that what I was about to discuss was something that could provide them with a three to five per cent change in performance. It may appear insignificant, but when you think back on that 10,000-metre race, it can be huge!

I told them that altitude training is what would take them to the next level of their performance; the research was unequivocal. I talked at length about the physiological benefits of altitude training. I elaborated on the risks associated with it and how we could prevent altitude sickness or overtraining from occurring. I discussed my experience with swimmers leading into the Sydney Olympics and how it had so positively influenced their preparation and performance.

As we've seen, altitude training has been instrumental for the team—it's one of the additional programs that made a difference, just like the icing on the cake, between ordinary athletes and champions.

David—Jack Daniels and altitude training

In 2005 Jack Daniels was in Flagstaff, Arizona, as the head coach for middle- and long-distance running at Northern Arizona University. I got him to speak to the playing group about altitude training. Jack was a two-time Olympian and medal-winner in the modern pentathlon and he had coached a number of elite athletes, from milers Jim Ruyn and Mary Slaney, to marathoners Joan Benoit and Jerry Lawson. He had an extensive background in elite sport and research in exercise physiology; he was the NCAA (National Collegiate Athletic Association) 'National Coach of the Year' three times and was also named the NCAA 'Coach of the Century'.

I introduced Jack to the playing group and outlined his achievements. They were all ears. His demeanour was laidback, like his Texan drawl, but he also presented an air of confidence for a man in his early seventies. He immediately got the group laughing when he said, 'I am Jack Daniels from Texas, not the one from Tennessee.'

He introduced the benefits of altitude training to the boys by pointing out that many, many athletes have demonstrated significant improvement in their performance after using it. These athletes had gone on to continue to perform personal bests for weeks, months and even years after their last visit to altitude.

'After all, dealing with adversity, mental stress and physical stress are all important lessons to learn on the way to championship athletic performances,' Jack said. 'I have avoided a declaration that altitude training leads to improved physiological performance parameters, but I have concluded that training at altitude does not make you a worse performer. I have never found a subject in all of my altitude-training research who believes his or her time with us was a negative experience. The athletes never complained of losing fitness abilities or becoming a lesser athlete; on the contrary, many said they were happy they participated. That's good enough for me.

'Your experience at altitude training,' he continued, 'will not only improve you, it will stay with you for life. Training at altitude can hurt, often more than similar training at sea level and that is something that is planted in your memory bank for life!'

CHAPTER 3

OPERATIONS

The idea of working at a football club seems glamorous to many fans. They are intrigued by all the intricacies of the life. They want to know all about their heroes, especially what they are really like as people. Footy fanatics are fascinated by footy-related gossip in the media and want to know every detail about the current list of players, injuries, game structures and the season's potential for success. Somewhere in their brains, too, are pieces of advice they'd like to share and perhaps even suggestions they think the club may not have thought of.

To those passionate about football, a football club is revered above all other things. The truth is that a football club is like any other workplace and it has a business model similar to that of many other successful businesses. There are employees and there is a hierarchical structure, with managers and department heads. Performance is measured by productivity. If the business underperforms, then areas are scrutinised and conclusions drawn. These results can lead to changes in structure, management or personnel.

The one major difference, however, between a football club and other kinds of business is that so much of its operations are left open for the public to see. Television cameras, journalists and the public are privy to almost everything that goes on in the club's day-to-day operations. If not, then they demand to know and go searching for it. Your performance as an employee is not only judged by your superiors, but also by the general public, who, as passionate fans, feel they have the right to know and comment.

Mick—The media

In 2005, AFL CEO Andrew Demetriou publicly criticised the Sydney Swans and its then coach, Paul Roos. The media was all over it.

Demetriou insisted that the Swans game plan, which included the overly defensive tactic of flooding—congesting the opposition's forward half to minimise scoring options—and high-possession offence—retaining the ball through chip kicks until a scoring opportunity presents itself—was 'unattractive' and 'ugly'.

The fuss escalated after Sydney's big loss to the in-form St Kilda in Round 10, when the league boss went as far as to predict that Sydney would never win a Premiership if it continued its current playing style. The Swans were labelled 'ugly ducklings' in the press.

I was a regular columnist with *The Australian* newspaper and I decided to use my article that week to voice my own opinion on the issue. I stressed that

Roos should 'stick to his guns' and ignore Demetriou's comments. I basically advised my coaching
counterpart to play whatever game best suited his
team. Roos expressed his appreciation in subse-
quent media interviews.

I'm sure he was strong enough to withstand the
storm and push on with his game plan without my
intervention. However, I wrote the article to provide
a colleague with some much-needed support and
that is exactly how it was accepted.

Sydney went on to win the Premiership that season, suffocating West Coast with their flood to grab
victory in a low-scoring grand final: 8.10 (58) to 7.12
(54).

Football media is the most saturated area of the
press, with at least two accredited AFL journalists
for every player in the competition. The scrutiny is
immense and, at times, overwhelming.

As a coach, I often avoid reading newspapers
or watching television news reports, thereby avoid-
ing the representation (or misrepresentation) of my
team or myself.

In the media, opinions come from all sources:
former coaches and players; journalists who live and
breathe the game but have never played it at an elite
level; and supporters. You would think this would
provide several different angles to every issue, but
it seems that, more often than not, once an agenda
is set everyone jumps on board with a similar view-
point and comments, thus escalating the issue to a
frenzy.

Think about the number of times a coach's
'head' has been called for in the media, forcing the

club to communicate a response. This media storm inevitably dies down when the coach is positively backed or the team's fortunes improve. The media then turns its attention to something or someone else. Remember, big news stories sell newspapers and increase television ratings!

While negotiating my final contract with Collingwood, I was called 'too old' and 'past it' in the press. Several journalists suggested my best was behind me and that Collingwood should move on with another coach. This was far from the first time the media had predicted my demise!

Less than two years later we won the Premiership. The players and staff of the club, including me, were hailed as heroes. All of a sudden my worth increased and I was the doyen of coaching. At 57 and the oldest coach to win a Premiership, I was no longer 'old', I was 'experienced'. The change in attitude amused me greatly.

When you're the subject of media outpourings you don't view the press the same way as an outsider does. The general public can pick up a newspaper, read a report, form an opinion and move on. As the target, you have to live with the questions, interrogations, perceptions and presumptions. There's no escaping it.

As a public figure representing an organisation, press conferences are compulsory. Therefore, responding to press—negative or positive—is unavoidable. If journalists ever take any kind of response as validation of their reports, they shouldn't.

The media does not drive a football club or the people in it. While the press can be very powerful as a collective, it is the readers, viewers and listeners that will be swayed by particular stories, not the people being written about.

I can categorically say that I have never changed a game plan, dropped a player or left a club because of media suggestion, insinuation or intimidation. I have never felt compelled to do or not do something because a member of the press recommended that I should. Ask any AFL coach and I'm sure he will tell you the same. The media does not feed football, football feeds the media.

In saying this, I still acknowledge the importance of the press in the growth and sustained development of the AFL. I have actually become part of the media conglomeration, sought as an expert analyst by radio, television and newspapers and I enjoy this role.

The public has an insatiable appetite for football news and in the end the media feeds it. Win or lose, there will always be a headline.

Spokes in the wagon wheel

The key to a successful business is always to keep in mind that everyone is linked in some way. At a football club every person plays a part in the operation. At times there can be weaker links or even breakdowns. These can be supported by other departments to maintain day-to-day operations, so that the system keeps going and doesn't break down altogether. There are always stronger parts of the network, but each part plays its role.

Perhaps an easy way to appreciate this is by comparing it to a wagon wheel. The outer circle of the wheel plays a fundamental role in its function—if this circular shape wasn't there, and there were just spokes, the wheel would not turn smoothly and the spokes would get caught in the ground or even sink in the dirt. And if the spokes weren't there, the outer rim would have nothing to support it and it would not turn at all or collapse.

If, however, some of the spokes are broken or missing, the wheel can still turn, but not as efficiently. The wheel can't support the weight that it could if it had a full set of strong, well-made spokes. The wheel can also turn if the rim is dented or chipped, just not as smoothly or efficiently.

A football team is like a wagon wheel. A team could still play a game of football if the boot-studder lost their boots and they were forced to play in runners. But they wouldn't have the grip in wet conditions and thus wouldn't perform as well as their competitors in footy boots. If the head coach was sick and unable to coach, any of the assistant coaches could step into the role and the game would go on and the players would be guided through their four quarters. But the lack of consistency and tactical experience could destabilise the team and its performance.

Identifying your lieutenants

When you need a job done you seek the person you know can execute and complete the task well, the one who can demonstrate pragmatism under pressure. Whether it is a player or coach performing in big games or a manager leading his group when times are difficult, trust in one's own ability to perform and support the mission is vital. Unfortunately, along with the trusted performers, we also have, on the one hand, those who appease and are referred to as 'yes men' and on the other, those who disbelieve and confront, emanating negativity. Those who enhance the critical mass, support team-oriented goals and grow with the program are the true lieutenants.

Mick—Identifying leaders

Leaders are not always top-ranked players; nor are top-ranked players always great leaders.

In the 1970s the England cricket team was captained by Mike Brearley. He wasn't the greatest batsman (in fact, he was quite average) he couldn't bowl and he was slow in the field. As a leader, though, he was able to generate great enthusiasm and desire within a team that was given little hope of winning the Ashes on Australian soil. He gelled an outstanding group of young men together into the team that won the Ashes 3–0 in England in 1977 and then 5–1 in 1978–79 in Australia.

Compared to Mike, the great Ian Botham (who I have a lot of time for, both as a cricketer and for his social conscience) tormented Australia as a batsman and bowler. However, when he was appointed captain, he failed dismally. The weight of expectation was far too high and told on his bowling and batting, to the point that he lost the captaincy.

Whenever I was looking to appoint new leaders at a football club, if they hadn't already revealed themselves through their manner, their peer following or their desire, I would lock a group of senior players in a room and pose a particular question—this is the fastest and easiest way to identify a leader.

Inevitably, either a player would stand up and answer off his own back (identifying himself as a natural leader), or a player would stand up and answer for the group as a nominated leader. In this latter instance, there is almost always a 'silent leader' as well.

An example of this is Richmond throughout the 1960s, '70s and early '80s, when Graeme Richmond virtually controlled the club from behind the scenes. The presidents and the CEOs during those years may have fired the shots, but the gun was invariably loaded by Graeme.

It is extremely important to have appropriate leaders appointed to direct and guide teammates or workmates. The right leader will lead by example and by voice; they will ultimately win the respect of the group as a person of action. People will always follow their lead.

The wrong leader may mimic someone who is a good leader, but flaws will eventually appear in his makeup. If they are a 'do as I say, not as I do' leader, people will catch on and stop following. If they show indecision—fence-sitting—they will leave people with uncertainty.

I believe we got it right when appointing the following captains:

- Nick Maxwell was a standout, demonstrated by the way he worked his way from the rookie list onto the main list with exemplary behaviour, both on and off the ground. He's a wonderful, caring person for his teammates in their football and also the rest of their lives. His attitude was 'club first, self second', which made him an ideal candidate for the captaincy. He's the hardest worker on the field for his teammates' success. He doesn't need the ball to be a great captain. The players respect him for all these characteristics.

- Nathan Buckley, a brilliant player, also had experience to offer his younger Collingwood teammates. Totally driven to be the best, he set a fantastic but stern regime for his teammates to reach his level. In all of the games he played with the Pies, he was rarely without a tag, but he never complained. He just got on with the job. Nathan played the game to the rules, played to win and was deeply affected by failure.

- John Worsfold, a young captain, was chosen to lead West Coast because of his ability to lead by example on field. He was one of the toughest, most uncompromising players I've coached. He never feared the big tasks and never took a backward step. He, like the two above, had an insatiable appetite for success.

All of these men were as brilliant off-field as they were on-field as captains.

As a coach, having the right captain and leadership group provides extra support, extra direction and an extra voice of reason. It is fundamental to the success of any side. It forms the very foundation on which to build a team.

No leadership equals no long-term success.

Efficiency and productivity

In Australian Rules Football, teams need to share their workload throughout a game by rotating players on and off the interchange bench for the team to be able to sustain its level of intensity. The Tour de France is a good example of efficient and productive use of resources through planning and teamwork. The event comprises approximately 20 teams of nine riders performing over three weeks. As seen on television, many cyclists ride in one big group known as the *peloton*. Each team strategically protects the lead rider—a Lance Armstrong or a Cadel Evans—so he can slipstream behind his teammates and reduce his workload against the wind. The goal is that he will be strong in the final stages of the race, where he is required to produce higher workloads.

The cyclist who protects his lead rider is known as the *domestique*; his finishing position is less important than that of his leader. Among the domestique riders, a hierarchy exists comprising of *super-domestiques* (or lieutenants) and the dog soldiers who expend their energy blocking chasing moves when they have riders up the road in a position to win. The lieutenants remain with the leader as long as they can during the most demanding phases, before the lead rider makes his decisive attack to win the stage. They also bring bottles of water and bags of food from the team vehicles and shield teammates from opposing cyclists. They stop and help teammates with mechanical disasters or crashes and are prepared to sacrifice their bicycle or wheel for their leader. The groundwork laid by the domestiques plays an integral role in conserving the energy of the lead rider.

It is when the domestique riders don't meet the terms of their specific instructions and their work rate drops that the system breaks down and becomes inefficient—this could be likened to losing some spokes in the wagon wheel. These riders are still performing at an elite level but not as efficiently and this could be the difference between winning and losing a stage of the race—or worse still, the Tour de France.

All great athletes and teams have the ability to express a level of efficiency when performing and make it look easy to the onlooker while still being highly productive. Speed has improved in most sports over the years and will continue to improve. Sprinter Usain Bolt continues to break world records for the men's 100-metre event. Since the Russian swimmer Vladimir Salnikov broke the 15-minute barrier in the men's 1500-metre freestyle event in 1980, it has been further reduced by some 20 seconds.

The speed of AFL matches has increased over the years and it will continue to get faster. It is predominantly in the efficiency of the athlete's performance that the greatest improvements can occur. The management of time, the use of resources and the implementation of new methods all contribute to enhancing the performance of an athlete. The way an AFL team plays tactically can determine what energy output is generated, as well as imposing higher workloads on the opposition. Being on the right side of the energy ledger will often determine the result of the game.

David—Pushing the boundaries

In December 2005, at our last training session before Christmas, I planned to challenge the boys and identify who could stand up to the rigours of stress when they were up against it. It was a continuation of the preseason preparation, with holidays looming and an opportunity to test the squad physically and mentally.

The football component was planned to create a competitive emphasis that lasted two and a half hours. The gruelling one-on-one tackling and chasing depleted the player's energy levels. Two and a half hours of ball work and game-orientated drills, man on man, was clearly showing the survival of the fittest. We showed no empathy but just drove them forward into the abyss. They had given their all in what was an extremely arduous session. The next 60 minutes tested each individual's physical and mental resolve. High-intensity interval running is challenging at the best of times, but at the end of a mountain of ball work it's far from appetising to any athlete. Competitive 200-metre and 300-metre races were evenly matched with minimal rest—we never told them the exact number of repetitions they would be doing but just kept giving the command to get up to the line and execute the challenge.

The human body has a natural ability to go into autopilot and go through the motions, but when there's competition involved, people have an uncanny ability to dig deep and push the limits just a bit further. Elite athletes love competition and hate to lose.

We challenged the boys to complete a 500-metre time trial in under 1 minute and 45 seconds, which was quite achievable if they were fresh, but given the state they were in, success was highly unlikely. The last man's time was the one that would be measured. In their fatigued state, the boys showed hopelessness and despondency.

But then Nathan Buckley, Scott Burns, Jimmy Clement, Tarkyn Lockyer and Paul Licuria quickly rallied the boys into level-of-fitness groups, with the weaker athletes at the front and the stronger athletes at the rear. Paul and Tarkyn took up the rear and Nathan called out to Anthony Rocca, 'Don't let Lica catch you!' Their legs felt like jelly, their hearts were pumping, they were gasping for air but their vocal cords were hurling encouragement to the weaker athletes to strive for the set time.

At this stage, some players had withdrawn into self-preservation mode; fatigue can make cowards of us all. It was the players who were really up against it physically who drew upon some vestiges of inner strength to push themselves and others forward. They knew that if they achieved the set time, the 500-metre time trials would finish and they'd be given respite.

At the 400-metre mark, their heads were wobbling around, their running form swayed and the back-markers were onto them like lame dogs. The back-markers, who ran like gazelles, could have passed them quite easily and completed the time trial in well under the set time, but they decided to ease off their pace and push the slower players to the end. The sense of mateship and cohesion was alive and kicking. Every onlooker felt a sense of wonderment seeing how these individuals came together to achieve their task.

The last man collapsed over the line in 1 minute 43 seconds. They were sprawled and bellowing for air. I knew they were stretched to their limit, but I looked at Mick and was on the brink of pushing a bit further. I was just waiting for any sign of weakness.

It was just at that moment that Chris Egan asked, 'Do we have any more? Is that it?' Well, the simple response was known by all—never ask how many reps we're going to do. I replied roughly that they would do a few more! The boys erupted into fuming animals, wanting to attack Chris Egan and probably me too.

They lined up again for a 500-metre time trial and went again. They fell way below their target. At this stage they were humiliated as athletes and just hanging on for survival. We gathered them into a circle on the ground and six ten-kilogram medicine balls were allocated to individuals to do shoulder presses while every other player was directed to keep their hands high up in the air.

Their faces just displayed pain. Eyes clenched, nostrils flared and mouths screwed up as those with the medicine balls performed their shoulder presses while the others stood with their arms up, concentrating on coping with the burning sensation in their shoulders. I asked some of the players if they would like give to up. Tarks [Tarkyn Lockyer], a well-conditioned warrior who could tolerate most punishments meted out, showed signs of fragmenting; I found he was a great barometer of how the boys were travelling. Pushing them to their limits gave us an indication of how they would cope under pressure.

We gave them an early Christmas present, but more importantly, we gave them the ability to push their limits; when times got tough they could remember this experience and not give in. When fatigued, it's easy to curse your teammate, but the ones who encouraged others and remained committed to working as a team fired up when the chips were down.

Humour is so often used when people are exposed to the elements. At the completion of the session, Tarks came over said, 'Thanks for the Christmas present Butters, as well as my buck's present!' A few of the boys broke into a laugh. That night Tarks was having his buck's turn as he was getting married in early January.

Shane Wakelin also commented on the session, asking, 'What did that cost us Butters?' The standard reply was quickly echoed back that it was all for free—'Costs you nothing!'

The jovial responses by the boys indicated that the group were close, proud of their efforts and in good spirits, even though they were totally worn out. We put them under the blowtorch as a test—some melted whereas others kept it together.

Planning is everything

The success of a business also requires careful planning. Some events, however, are impossible to foresee. What becomes more important is not the unpredicted event itself but the way the team reacts to it.

In football the unexpected is very often injury. How could anyone predict that Nick Maxwell would receive such a bad blow in the 2011 NAB Cup semifinal that resulted in injuries to his liver and kidney? Nevertheless, consistency and sticking to the plan is very important. Yes, unexpected circumstances will arise—they always do—but the best and most desired scenario is to stick to the original game plan.

> *I tell this story to illustrate the truth of the statement I heard long ago in the Army: plans are worthless, but planning is everything. There is a very great distinction because when you are planning for an emergency you must start with this one thing: the very definition of*

'emergency' is that it is unexpected, therefore it is not going to happen the way you are planning.

Dwight Eisenhower

David—Grand Canyon 2010: Expect the unexpected

We had been meandering down the Grand Canyon South Kaibab trail for three hours, descending at a brisk pace. Suddenly I heard a whistle! 'Tony, that's the emergency signal!' I exclaimed to our club doctor, Tony Page. 'Let's move quickly!' Before the hike we'd planned to break the party into two groups and enable some of the less conditioned players and staff to start before the more hardened players and staff. Each group leader was to carry a whistle, only to be used in case of an emergency. This had been our fifth trip to the Grand Canyon as a group and we felt everyone was well equipped to handle the terrain.

The Grand Canyon can actually be deadly—there are several fatalities each year. On our initial trip in 2005, we were strongly urged by the park ranger not to attempt a same-day descent to the Colorado River and ascent. He told us it would take our group 14 hours to complete and he warned us, 'You'll need lanterns and warm clothing to deal with the temperature dropping later in the evening. I repeat, do not attempt it, Sir!'

After such a warning, Mick, Neil Balme and I deliberated on the pros and cons of attempting the trek. We had travelled by bus for two hours to get there and we were determined to complete the task, but not at the risk of any of our party. It had been difficult to persuade the club to allow us to go, so imagine if one of our players suffered a serious injury! After considerable discussion and strategic planning, we felt confident and well prepared and decided to go. We outlined the risks to the group and told them that it would be a challenge, but if they worked together we believed they were capable of accomplishing the trek. We completed it successfully in just over seven hours and were delighted that we had no injuries.

In 2010, the players who had completed the canyon challenge before were not overly excited to do it again; they knew what an arduous and challenging trek it is.

You can complete the descent without too much difficulty. But it's the ascent that involves trekking switchbacks (a term the locals use for the hairpin bends in the meandering track). The climb back up is 15 kilometres with a 1500-metre elevation. The last three to four hours are a continual gradient with the climber entering back into altitude (almost 2500 metres). It's the last two to three hours that hit most people hard. Because our group was alternating between running and walking for the last 10 kilometres, their resolve and spirit were very quickly tested.

No wonder they were not jumping up and down with joy when they knew they were going back into the canyon of pain!

Luke Ball—Grand Canyon 2010
I don't think my legs have never ached like that before. I was spent.

David—Grand Canyon 2010 (continued)

On your initial descent you're overwhelmed by the Canyon's sheer size. Its intricate and colourful landscape is spectacular for the first five to ten minutes. But once the groups have settled into their rhythmic marching gait, eyes are lowered to your footing and become transfixed on the heels of the person immediately in front.

Each time we do the canyon climb, we carry a defibrillator in case of an emergency. We had very precious cargo in the form of the club's greatest assets—professional footballers—as well as the staff. We also had paid executives in our party who wanted to experience an altitude training camp with their beloved Collingwood footballers.

There were five team members who were trained to use the defibrillator and to handle emergency first-aid situations. Among these, Dr Greg Shuttleworth was assigned to the first party and Dr Tony Page to the second group. Tony and I responded quickly to the whistle and moved swiftly down towards the source of the alarm. In those few seconds, several scenarios ran through my mind. What if one of the players was critically injured or had even gone over the edge? I also envisaged the worst scenario of all, a loss of life. I thought I was prepared for any condition this player, whoever he may be, would be in.

We got there within five minutes. As we often say, expect the unexpected. To my surprise, it was not a player but Dr Greg Shuttleworth. He was grimacing in pain and looking extremely grey, lying on his back with our physiotherapist, Dave Francis, kneeling by his side. Tony and I quickly glanced at each other and knew we were thinking the same thing—that Greg was having a heart attack. I asked Greg how he was going and he replied, 'I've broken my leg!' Greg's the head of the emergency ward at a country base hospital so we didn't question his diagnosis. He was coping really well, but we could tell he was going into shock.

The players were gathering around. Unlike game day, when they rarely see the medical team go into action because they're playing or coming on and off the field and distracted by the game's events, this was very confronting. They were anxious and waiting to see how things were going to pan out. Would they be expected to finish now there was an emergency on their hands? Or would the trek be aborted in order to help Greg?

Tony started to deal with Greg, while Dave Francis assisted by initiating our automatic emergency procedures. This was their domain and they were in full control of the situation. I instructed Mike Smith, one of our altitude training camp coordinators, to run down to the ranch at the bottom by the Colorado River to seek help. It was approximately five kilometres away. Although we had elite athletes in our midst, Mike was the best choice, as he was an All-American college distance runner who knew the area very well. I told him to contact the ranger and obtain a stretcher. The first group had already broken off and was heading down to the Colorado for recovery, unaware what had happened to Greg. I discussed the situation with the medical team and decided it would be best for me to lead the remainder of our party on and meet up with the rest of the group. Time was not to be wasted.

Tony and Dave continued to provide support to Greg, immobilised the injury and controlled his pain. Our aim was to support him but also to keep the group together and fresh. In the back of my mind I thought we may have to stretcher him out of the canyon and who better to take on this task but a young healthy team of athletes? I needed them fresh and in good shape if this was to occur.

As the players emerged at the base of the canyon by the Colorado River, they were recovering and revitalising their legs. I told Mick what had happened and we began planning our next steps. We had a party of 45 on the trek, so I gathered the strongest to help with the stretcher. Some were players (such as Travis Cloke, Darren Jolly, Cameron Wood and Shane McNamarra), but I also included staff members Paul Licuria, Justin Crow and Mick Dugina because I knew I could completely rely on them to undertake any task asked of them and follow instructions without question.

Mike Smith brought the ranger and a stretcher. The ranger decided that we should get a chopper to pick up Greg and take him straight to hospital. We had to transport him down to the chopper landing pad, which was about four kilometres away. We had six people carrying the stretcher and another four delegated to rotate in when required.

We arrived at the landing pad and by this stage Greg was stable and was becoming embarrassed about what had happened. The boys kept their sense of humour and gave him a bit of banter, 'Geez Doc, you've slowed us. Does that mean we can get a ride up to the top in the chopper?'

As we had discussed the night before, if we were expecting a mishap, it would be with one of the executives we had brought with us, or even a player. But we honestly did not factor in that our injured party member could be our own doctor.

Carrying a stretcher loaded with an injured person appears quite easy, but after four kilometres on sloping, uneven ground I realised how challenging it was and how much I had asked of these men and what great fortitude and integrity they showed in completing it. I felt very proud of their selfless efforts.

Despite Greg's fall, a breakaway party of 15 to 20 players completed the trek in well under seven hours. Mick and the other coaching staff led the remaining group back. Greg got to the hospital safely and another Grand Canyon trek was accomplished.

Heat of the battle: Drawn grand final

The Collingwood Football Club was put through one of its greatest mental tests following the 2010 drawn grand final. Both St Kilda and Collingwood went into the grand final with the belief and assumption that one team would be defeated and one team would be victorious. The possibility of a draw was something that was barely considered.

David—The drawn grand final

As in every other game of football, each staff member and player in the drawn grand final of 2010 between Collingwood and St Kilda was totally absorbed in their role and working diligently to deliver their responsibilities to their best of their ability. I was no different to anyone else. I was scanning the monitor on the laptop, viewing the game time, delivering feedback to the coach's box, encouraging exhausted players to leave nothing in the tank and to be ready to go back on when called, reminding others to keep focussed, all while watching the game.

With a minute to go, the arm-wrestle was locked, the tension was great and the crowd was deafening, but down on the bench it was still business as usual with everyone executing their jobs as well as they could. Even though the crowd's roar was deafening and the tension on the bench was pulsating, depleted players found the inner strength to bark encouragement and direction to their teammates.

The time clock was descending rapidly and our opportunity to convert a score was quickly evaporating. The Saints had momentum and we were fighting for survival. I continued to remain in operational mode, subconsciously knowing that it was all the more important that I remained calm and focussed; it was imperative that I kept my head in the crisis. With less than three seconds to go it was clear that a drawn grand final was upon us. The siren sounded and the players numbly sprawled on the ground displaying fatigue and a sense of hopelessness.

I had a vivid flashback—there I was, a 13-year-old boy hearing the final siren in the drawn grand final between Collingwood and North Melbourne in 1977. Like everyone in the crowd, I watched in bewilderment and wondered what was going to happen next. I turned to my dad and fired questions at him. I asked him if there was going to be a replay and if I would get to go again. I saw the coach of Collingwood, Tom Hafey, coming down from the coach's box and the players sitting on the ground with their heads in their hands, bleak faces showing despair.

In that split-second I had an epiphany: it suddenly occurred to me that our players were doing the same thing. Like me, all those years ago, the crowd wanted answers. I knew I had to remind these players, that, like me, they had a responsibility. Their job was not yet finished. I rushed across to a group of players who were on the ground and yelled at them, 'Come on! Get the fuck up!' The sounding of the siren had allowed them the right to fall into a state of completion, yet the job wasn't completed. For some it fell on deaf ears, while others started to gather and congregate.

Unbeknown to me, whilst I was still gathering my thoughts about the process for the following week, the Norm Smith Medal presentation was about to commence. During this time Mick, Geoff Walsh, Nick Maxwell, Eddie McGuire and I gathered to discuss the course of events. There were so many things to consider: a replay, recovering from the game, the grand final dinner, a press conference, drug-testing and more. But first and foremost, I was focussing on rejuvenating and restoring the players' wellbeing. There were so many permutations. I remember saying to Mick that we should not make any decision in haste. I knew that we should get the players to rehydrate, refuel and do their recovery interventions as we would after any other game.

Eddie described to us how, after the drawn grand final of 1977, North Melbourne had gone back to their post-game event and shared it with their families. He told us that it had had a positive effect on the players. As much I was interested in this discussion and wanted to share the evening with my family, I knew that my responsibility was to the wellbeing of the players; I needed to bring as much normalcy as I could and remain pragmatic. I could sense players were hovering around our small group in anticipation, looking for leadership. Again, I went into automatic mode, brought them in together and began their recovery.

During this chaos there were moments when I was listening, but I was more interested in watching the body language of the St Kilda players. I noted their fatigue, but still with a level of buoyancy about them. They appeared collected, but Michael Gardiner seemed to be a beacon of despondency. I could tell from his body language, and that of those he was talking to, that he was carrying an injury that might limit his chances of playing the following week. It was later confirmed that he had torn his hamstring and was unable to play in the rematch.

As we walked across the ground a barrage of questions were fired at me. It didn't stop! Later, when I caught up with my family, the same questions were asked by my son. The shoe was now on the other foot—just like my dad 33 years ago, I was the one who had to provide the answers. There was an extra spring in my step as I relished the thought that this was a wonderful opportunity to be in another grand final and to live to fight another day.

This was further confirmed the next morning as the players, Mick Dugina and I walked around the Melbourne Botanical Gardens track (known as the Tan) as part of their recovery. Our upbeat, much-loved Dale Thomas was able to ease the tension with his antics. He entertained us by sneaking up on cameramen and photographers in a 'Mr Bean' manner. The tension had broken and we were enjoying each other's company. We were back on track in our quest for the Premiership cup.

Mick—The drawn grand final

Given that it had only happened twice before in history, no one was prepared for a draw. Looking back, it's no wonder everyone was so shocked. Holidays were booked for the following week (by players, coaches and AFL officials, not to mention the punters) and I can't speak for Ross Lyon, the St Kilda coach, but a draw was the last thing on my mind as we headed into a grand final.

As the ball was kicked to St Kilda's half-forward flank in the final minute, the only thing I could think was, 'This has to be closed down.' I could see the clock in the coach's box and the only available scenario left in the time remaining was for the Saints to kick long and mark inside fifty for a shot at goal. Locking down the stoppage was our only hope. We held it in and time ran out. We had just forced the third drawn grand final in VFL/AFL history.

Unbeknown to us, a sewerage problem had left our change rooms flooded during the final quarter, so as we began to leave the field an AFL official told us we had to go the spare rooms on the other side of the ground.

Familiarity was what we needed at this stage and a change of rooms wasn't it. The players were already emotionally and physically distressed and now they were also disoriented.

There was a lot of chatter about what should happen next, with even a hint that time-on may still be played. My main concern was the welfare of our playing group. Collingwood's football operations manager, Geoff Walsh, took care of the peripheral matters as David and I planned what would be in the players' best interests.

As we walked into the Great Southern Stand change rooms it was as if a stun grenade had gone off. The players scattered. With their socks down they sat leaning against the walls, unable to speak. I looked around the room and it was obvious that not one player had control of the matter in his mind, that no one had managed to make sense of the situation. They were looking for answers and direction.

We had to remain calm. Drawing from my experience of a drawn semifinal with West Coast in 2007, I knew we had to be decisive. The playing group had only to worry about playing again; they didn't need to worry about things that shouldn't concern them.

My first impulse was to finish the game by finishing the night. Historically, the competing clubs have post-grand final functions organised where family and friends gather to celebrate or commiserate. I felt the only way to conclude the game was to proceed with our dinner as planned and give everyone the opportunity to open up with friends and family.

I thought I'd get a good response, so I asked the boys, 'Who wants to go to tonight's dinner?' but not one hand was raised. Had I totally misread the situation? Then I asked who didn't want to go to the dinner and again no one raised a hand. This was a clear indication that the players needed a leader at that moment and whatever decision was made would be the one they would follow.

I believed it right that we should still go to the dinner. I'm sure there was some resistance to this, but there was enough support to back this decision.

It was an early night without alcohol. There were speeches, though instead of being reflective, they were positive reinforcements of what was to come. The players freed themselves of the pent-up emotion of the game by talking it out with their loved ones. They cleansed their souls, so to speak.

By Sunday morning we'd 'finished' the game. While publicly I called it half-time, Grand Final 1 had ended for us. We were only looking ahead now. At the recovery session the boys had a laugh and the mood lifted. It was so important they didn't feel the need to bear the weight of the world.

There would be no typical AFL grand final lead-up this time—no Brownlow or city parades—so it was back to normality. We could prepare ourselves the way we'd always done. After the game, the ball was handed to Walshy to take care of the logistics of a second grand final week, and then it was passed to David to get the players physically ready. It was up to the coaches to digest all the available information and prepare for the opposition, again.

By the Monday we were well on the way to being ready to play the second grand final.

Scott Pendlebury—Drawn grand final

Two days before the grand final I was getting sick and I thought it was just nerves as I couldn't eat very much. The day before the game I was nauseous and vomited throughout the day. I realised it wasn't nerves; it was a bug I'd picked up. I did everything I could to prepare for the game, but by the end of the second quarter I was drained. At the end of the game I was just shattered, physically and mentally exhausted. While Mick spoke to us after the game in the rooms I was light-headed and was holding on, trying not to be sick. Straight after he spoke to us I ran into the toilets and vomited. I went to the function that night, spent time with family and friends and got my focus back on track.

Luke Ball—Drawn grand final

I got my hamstring right throughout the week. I built up the game too much—particularly because we were playing against my old team. At the end of the game I was relieved as I knew we had a second chance and that I could prepare properly for the next game. The function that night was positive and gave me an opportunity to spend time with my family and friends, whereas if given the choice, I would have just stayed at home and internalised the game.

Permanence, perseverance and persistence in spite of all obstacles, discouragement and impossibilities: It is this, that in all things distinguishes the strong soul from the weak.

Thomas Carlyle

CHAPTER 4

BALANCE

Too much of anything affects your equilibrium

People often talk about stress to express how they are feeling when they are overworked, overloaded or just not coping with external stimuli such as work, family, financial issues or other pressures. In the past the word stress was used to describe metals when they are put under intense pressure. Descriptions of feeling anxious, tired, constantly worried, depressed and having no energy are all ways that individuals may describe their overall wellbeing at such times. What the body is actually experiencing in these circumstances is physiological, psychological and emotional tension—generally as a result of overload. What has occurred is an *imbalance* in their *equilibrium*. It could be that they are working longer hours than they are recreating (recovering) or the reverse. An imbalance has occurred.

Mick—The 1992 Grand Final

It's fairly normal for sporting teams to be 'gung ho' before a game. Slapping, bumping and making noise can all be part of pre-game rev-up. However, I believe it's actually counterproductive to use too much energy before a game. All members of a team are individuals and will respond differently to the stimuli around them. Too much action or noise can be distracting to some, while not enough will leave others flat. I'm not saying the change room needs to be like a church or a library before the game, but the point is to maximise one's efforts, so 'noise with meaning' and a more controlled warm-up might actually produce better results.

Before the 1992 grand final, as we (West Coast) stood in the race waiting to enter the arena, I remember looking over to our opponents, Geelong. A very well-built Barry Stoneham was bumping his hip and shoulder against the concrete race wall with a steely look of determination on his face. The rest of the Geelong team was just as animated and over the top. Pumped up, they were extremely vocal, jumping and running on the spot, bouncing off each other, punching and jabbing the air. They were right up, as though on the edge of a big performance and totally ready for action.

I thought to myself, 'Geez, this could be a tough start.' Although I had expected it, I couldn't believe how fired up they were. In 1989, many of the same players had participated in what was dubbed 'the Battle of '89'—one of the toughest and hardest-fought grand finals in VFL history. Hawthorn beat the Cats by six points.

At the Eagles, we had experienced our own pain in the 1991 grand final, also losing to Hawthorn (but by 53 points), so we had something to prove that day too. However, our warm-up on this day seemed subdued compared to Geelong's. We were still animated, but I had worked on the theory that with such a big gap between warming up in the rooms and actually running out onto the ground (the staging for the pre-game entertainment had to be deconstructed and cleared away), there was no point wasting valuable energy too early. Instead, we ensured that the players stayed focussed on the task at hand with a calmer approach.

But when the game actually started I began to wonder if this had been the right tactic—Geelong practically bolted out of the blocks. We lost Don Pyke early to concussion and several other players, on the receiving end of some heavy knocks, were bruised and battered. By quarter time Geelong had a lead of 18 points and all the momentum.

At the break, club runner (and great friend) Rob Wiley, selector Ian Miller and I repeated the 'gather yourself' message to the boys as I wondered how much they had left in them. We had a good record against the Cats (having beaten them as recently as the semifinal by 38 points), but they were up and about and making us nervous.

By two-thirds of the way through the second quarter Geelong had us 8 goals to 4. Then two things happened that changed the course of the game.

Craig Turley was getting well beaten by Paul Couch in the centre, allowing the 1989 Brownlow Medallist to have too much influence on the game.

We needed to make a change. There is (usually) no next week in a grand final, so I had to be calculated and decisive. We moved Brett Heady, who had played as a half-forward flanker all year and was coming off a hamstring strain, onto Couch and he immediately quelled Couch's effect, as we'll see in further detail in Chapter 7.

In a team or group situation you have to be able, under pressure, to maintain focus on the team structure. Tony Evans, the quiet achiever of the squad in only his second season, single-handedly brought a sensible attitude back into the team to settle the players' nerves. Pyke's return to the field also had a settling influence and all of a sudden our natural game was creeping back in. We managed to bridge the gap to 12 points by the main break and gain the momentum.

Geelong was still vocal and aggressive and our players had also begun to get a bit over-the-top in the excitement of a fightback, so we used the break to settle them back down. The fact that we were trailing was an added incentive and helped us to once again focus on the job at hand. We needed to be role- and result-driven and too much excitement would not help.

As the two sides emerged from their respective races for the third term I noticed that Geelong looked a little drained. I felt immediately comforted knowing we had energy left to give as well as a fresh focus on the task.

We kicked five goals to one in the third quarter and took charge of the game.

Our big-game performers stood up—Peter Matera, Guy McKenna, John Worsfold, Peter Sumich,

Glen Jakovich and Evans and Pyke. Although we had just four goal-kickers for the match, it was a shared effort across the ground that led to our 28-point win.

No matter what the challenge, you must stay composed. The lion's roar will only scare you, it will not kill you. Geelong's roar before our clash showed exuberance and true aggression. We took a couple of big shots early and had to come back from behind, but we stuck to our game plan and structure and what we knew best. The on-field leaders shouldered the responsibility and that filtered through the entire list. By the end, we had more men that played well than Geelong had; we kept our composure and won.

To play a team sport you have to be emotional and passionate, but not misdirected. Tony Evans didn't get caught up in the razzamatazz of the occasion. Through solid work and direction he brought the focus back to winning the game.

Uncommon things happen on the big stage—like in a grand final. When teams or individuals succeed or fail there, the question is asked: 'Where was their focus?'

In elite sport or business you can't afford to be compromised by surrendering any of your energy. It's hard enough to beat an opponent with a full complement of energy. So keeping some in reserve and focussing it where it's needed most can only be beneficial.

Any athlete who functions in an intense and dynamic environment can be vulnerable to losing equilibrium. As AFL footballers are continually challenged (both physically and mentally) throughout preseason training and the football season itself, like all athletes they become susceptible to breaking down. So often the cumulative load of stress can create an imbalance and affect the holistic functioning of an athlete and cloud their specific focus.

The Manchester United player George Best is an example of how the life of an athlete can become unbalanced when one area dominates. In Georgie's case, it was alcohol. He became an alcoholic; this curtailed his career and eventually contributed to his death.

Another example is Australian Rules football's Ben Cousins. By his own admission, Ben became unbalanced when too much of one thing became dominant in his life: drugs. The difference in Ben's case was that he recognised this imbalance and worked to address it in order to return to being the champion athlete he had once been.

The many great athletes who have consistently performed at a very high level for a prolonged period of time have all lived a balanced life. These athletes have been able to sustain a strong work ethic while simultaneously managing myriad other aspects.

What, then, is the magic formula for a balanced life? There are many influences that can upset the equilibrium. However, it is possible for one to stay balanced by consistently maintaining wellbeing in four crucial areas: physical, mental, social and spiritual.

Physical

It's not possible to provide here a description of the ideal elite athlete's training program because they are all so varied, according to their specific sport. But the importance of physical activity for the body must be acknowledged. It is common knowledge that an active lifestyle decreases the likelihood of a variety of illnesses, particularly heart disease and diabetes. In order to have a balanced life, physical activity is crucial, but it must be properly tailored to the individual. For example, a middle-aged, overweight person commencing an exercise program may begin with a daily walk and gentle stretching, while an elite marathon runner may run in excess of a hundred kilometres a week.

Delivering the correct dose of training to an athlete is crucial for a positive outcome. Conversely, ill-informed athletes or coaches who set the wrong dose of training can have a detrimental effect on both the athletes' and the team's performance. The human body has a unique ability to respond to stress and adapt to the stimuli it receives. Through rest periods the body restores and adaptations occur. Put simply, too much work and too little rest is a recipe for disaster for an athlete. The process of identifying what the athlete can tolerate enables the athlete to push their boundaries in suitable increments and progress to achieve greater goals. Excessive adjustments can create an imbalance and jeopardise the athlete's chance of reaching their full potential.

Too much or too little of anything—sleep, food, weight training, endurance training, competition, cross-training or rest—can disturb the equilibrium. John Blakey was a dual Premiership player with North Melbourne who received little kudos outside of the Kangaroos. He was a thorough professional. He knew intuitively what his body could and could not tolerate and this enabled him to achieve consistency in his preparation and performance. A common phrase he would use while he was at the Kangaroos was, 'You are what you eat,' meaning that what you put into your body (and further, what you put into your training) will deliver rewards if you do it in a well-balanced way.

Blakey's percentage of body fat was extremely low for an athlete during the mid-1990s (this was not as common as it is today). His minimal body-fat levels were a direct reflection of what he consumed and how he trained. His regimented approach was successful, yet he still remained open to change. In the end, his own understanding of how his body coped with various stresses enabled him to maintain his fitness levels for 18 seasons of VFL/AFL football. He retired at 36 years of age after playing 359 games.

To be able to play this many games would indicate that he had few injuries. Sometimes injuries are due to bad luck, but the importance of simply looking after your body is often underestimated. Alcohol and athletes is not just a bad combination in relation to the antics they can get up to socially. The combination of recovering from strenuous performance—where the body is in a fatigued state or even slightly injured—with alcohol is not the ideal recipe for recovery. John treated his body like a temple and much of his longevity as a player can be attributed to his respect for the opportunity to play elite sport. He embraced the lifestyle of an elite athlete in all areas.

Mental

Mental, in this context, refers to two components: intellectual and psychological. The former is more easily defined as knowledge, while the latter can be thought of as emotional.

An elite athlete is so well trained that when a coach tells them to perform a particular training drill, they perform it without question. It's desirable, however, for the athlete to understand the mechanism behind the training drill (how and why it will benefit them) as well as its benefits, in order to better perform it. This doesn't mean that all athletes must have a sports-science background, but simply that some knowledge and understanding of physiology will help them train better. Such understanding is often an important contributor to the athlete's performance.

In the latter part of the 2009 season, Scott Pendlebury fractured his fibula. He underwent surgery to accelerate his recovery: the surgeon, Julian Feller, attached a plate to his fibula. An aggressive rehabilitation program was prescribed in order for him to attempt to play in the finals later that season. His progress was more advanced than had been expected and he was on target to play in the club's preliminary final against Geelong. After meeting the criteria and testing successfully, he went on to a full training session with the whole team. During this training session, however, he realised that he lacked power in his leg and the plate was pressing on his fibula and causing pain. He decided he was unfit to play. Because Scott understood and spoke up about what was hindering his performance, further injury was avoided.

The mental component being discussed here is not just about knowledge and understanding. It also encompasses an array of psychological characteristics—from anxiety to over-arousal. Successful athletes should acquire the ability to control these extremes. Just as they are finely tuned physically, they must also be trained mentally to cope with unexpected, extrinsic influences that may compromise performance.

In the 2004 Olympic Games, Grant Hackett competed in the 1500-metre freestyle event. He was suffering from a respiratory problem with a partially collapsed lung; it was reported that he had 25 per cent less lung-capacity. Astonishingly, he won this gruelling event. Most attributed this to sheer willpower.

Alan Didak is a highly skilled player for Collingwood. In 2006, he won the club's best and fairest award, the Copeland Trophy. He also received an All Australian honour that year and in the 2010 season. Alan is much more than what these awards represent, however. He is regarded as a vital offensive cog in the Collingwood team. He is opportunistic and is able to create things out of nothing and encourage his teammates to lift their own game. Alan was a vital component in the 2010 Collingwood finals team.

Unfortunately, on the eve of the finals, in the second-last game of the season, while playing against Adelaide, Alan ruptured the chest muscle known as the pectoralis major. This loomed as a potential season-ending injury. It was Alan's tenth season; he had played over 150 games and been involved in the 2002 and 2003 losing grand finals. His professional approach throughout the year had been outstanding, but his dream of playing in another grand final was evaporating very rapidly. His limited range of movement and loss of strength was evident. After the Adelaide game, Alan was despondent and stated that his injury wasn't looking too good. Recovery strategies were put into place immediately and surgery was discussed and Alan kept a buoyant hope that his finals campaign might still be alive.

Over the following days, Alan's confidence grew and surgery was looking less likely. He worked diligently on his rehabilitation and was able to get to a stage of having only slightly inhibited performance. Knowing that his muscle was fully ruptured and the pain was difficult, he continued to push on to support the team. He displayed a high level of positivity and deflected any attention from media, players and competitors about the status of his shoulder.

Alan demonstrated his resolve over this five-week period—he *believed* he would play—which consequently enabled him to train and perform at a high level. This belief in his recovery, combined with the proper medical and fitness interventions and understanding the importance of his role in the team, culminated in him taking part in a winning Premiership against the odds.

In the early stages of his career, Alan had doubted his own abilities and questioned his ability to overcome injuries. He's had a tumultuous career and has been exposed to some difficulties outside of the club. However, over this time, he achieved a self-assurance and a strong conviction that he could overcome adversity and setbacks. Alan not only achieved every footballer's dream of winning a Premiership, but he won a personal battle to develop self-worth.

So many athletes are tested with obstacles. Alan's injury was overcome principally through his mental resilience. The expectations of high-level competition can fragment many athletes. Adding the pressure of an injury can increase stress significantly, distract focus and compromise performance. Alan showed that if you go beyond the obstacles and believe in your capabilities, you will achieve.

First-year players in their initial AFL season frequently have difficulty seeing their own potential. They watch with awe as the likes of Dane Swan bench-press double their own maximum weight. It's hard for them to believe that they will be capable of lifting significantly greater weights, running faster time trials and achieving greater muscle mass.

But it should be remembered that players such as Dane were not always bench-pressing such weights or running impressive times. As the old saying goes, 'Rome wasn't built in a day'. When Dane Swan initially arrived at Collingwood, he lacked athletic prowess. Like many young players, he was unaware of how far he could go and what he could achieve. There was a potential resonating in him that he may have been unaware of. At some stage through his training, performance and personal life, a transformation occurred where he began to see changes in himself. As he matured he placed greater belief in the program, in his coaches and—more importantly—in himself. This success enabled Dane to see that he still had the potential to reach and achieve even greater goals. This approach became a self-fulfilling winning formula.

Dane Swan—A shift

In my early days at Collingwood I was going nowhere really. I was just floating through. Then I had my wake-up call. I thought I was invincible but I was knocked back on my arse. Now my mentality has shifted. I wanted to play well and return the favour to my family and my club. I wanted my parents to be proud of me. I love my lifestyle and I appreciate where I am because I nearly lost it. I am so lucky now and I have learnt a lot.

Young players who achieve results beyond their wildest dreams can often attribute this success to modelling themselves on players such as Dane. They begin to believe that they too may be capable of greatness and follow the process that the likes of Dane use. Just as Dane would have watched players like Nathan Buckley, Jimmy Clement and Paul Licuria in his early years, younger players are now watching him and learning from him.

Belief is nourished through small achievements, self-talk and sound processes. In the end, we like to foster a view that anything is achievable. If an athlete wants to achieve their maximum potential, it's essential that they have an absolute belief in themselves. There is no room for doubt.

It's the repetition of affirmations that leads to belief. And once that belief becomes a deep conviction, things begin to happen.

Muhammad Ali

Social

'All work and no play makes Jack a dull boy,' they say. Just as in any serious pursuit, time out to have fun and relax is necessary. Unfortunately, over time, some athletes have attracted negative publicity in social settings. Such things are not what is meant here by encouraging players to enjoy their social life. Supportive family networks and trusted friends can provide a healthy social environment to vent and forget the pressures of professional sport.

Over many years, hundreds of Collingwood players have had their families behind them, celebrating their sporting highs as well as having someone to fall back on when times have been difficult. These occasions can be weekly occurrences to players, or even daily. Within one day a regular senior player can find himself suddenly not selected because his style of play doesn't suit the upcoming opponent's different game plan; he'll have to work his hardest to find his place in the team again. Or he can go from playing one of the greatest games of his career to injuring himself so severely that he may be unavailable for the remainder of a season—or even his career.

In 2006, Blake Caracella's career came to a standstill prematurely when he suffered a fractured vertebra and spinal bruising. Blake recognised that the incident could have been catastrophic, so according to his doctors' recommendation, he retired to prevent the potential of paralysis. He knew that his family had supported his successes over his career. Now they were his priority and in such a crucial decision, they equally supported his choice to retire.

When playing sport at such a high level, the role of family and friends should never be taken for granted, because they are the reason that many athletes have achieved the success they have. Family and friends can provide support and—more importantly—keep you grounded. After all, these will be the people who will be there at the end of your career. A supportive family should not only be encouraged but also celebrated, for it is this support that can provide a player with important strength and courage, not only in sport but also in other aspects of life.

Brad Dick—Homesick

I'm close to my family. My uncle and a very close friend passed away during 2010, I wasn't playing footy due to an injury and I was homesick. But after seeing my mates play in a Premiership, I wanted to have a real crack and do it again next season, so I decided to stay in Melbourne. My family are really supportive of this decision.

Mick is a strong believer in players being able to spend special occasions, such as Christmas, weddings and other important events with family. At the end of each year, as players go their separate ways for the Christmas–New Year break, Mick always reminds his players of the importance of their family and friends. He tells them it's time to go home and give some time back to those who have supported them. The demands of football and the long season deprives families of their loved ones, so he encourages them to remember this and give a little back.

This was no more evident than in Marty Clarke's case— the first Irishman recruited by Collingwood. When he arrived he was put through an array of physiological and psychological tests. One of the first tests was a time trial around the Tan with David. The course is a 3.84 kilometre circuit, the majority of which has a slight downhill gradient. Anyone who knows this run would be familiar with Anderson Street, the most challenging part of the run as the steep uphill gradient is immediately confronting.

This test was to identify what type of endurance athlete Marty was. In the first 500 metres he ran at a cracking pace of approximately three and a half minutes per kilometre. David asked Marty if he liked running and Marty replied in his strong Celtic accent, 'I like to run! It's my time when I run.' As he progressed around the Tan, David expected that this Irishman wouldn't keep the pace up for much longer. But Marty kept the dialogue going and, astoundingly, he increased his pace up the Anderson Street hill. Most athletes have laboured breathing by this point, but Marty kept chatting in a relaxed state. He managed to complete the Tan well below a 13.30-minute time and appeared to be comfortable and in his element.

The next stage of his training tests incorporated a recovery swim. Marty was not so familiar with the water as the running track. When David told him to hop in the pool to aid his recovery from the run, he handed him a pair of flippers. Marty looked down at the flippers in astonishment and asked David what he should do with them.

It was a reminder to David that all athletes are individuals and that although Marty was an intelligent and gifted athlete, there were significant differences between their two worlds. Indeed, it was a lesson to all coaches to remember that no assumptions can be made and that all athletes are individuals. The jump from one's homeland to another is not to be taken lightly. Marty had made a huge leap leaving his familiar culture and adopting another.

His personality and quick wit and intellect made him very likeable. His continual references to his family, friends and girlfriend demonstrated his strong feelings for the green fields of home in Ireland. For Marty, leaving his loved ones to live in another country was a significant move. It's quite difficult for such players; they have to find new support groups because their family and friends are so far away.

In 2009, Marty's sister was getting married in the middle of the football season. He asked Mick if it would be at all possible for him to return home to Ireland and attend her wedding. Mick himself strongly values time with his own family. But in Marty's case, his family was on the other side of the world. Mick happily agreed to Marty going despite the potential ramifications of him missing two games. Mick realised the importance of such an occasion in a player's family and so Marty enjoyed his sister's wedding with his coach's blessing.

Nick Maxwell—On balance

You need to prioritise and manage. Erin, my wife, and my daughter, Milla, are number one. But footy at the moment also takes a very high priority. I don't waste time at the moment doing things that are irrelevant. Family and friends are important to me, so I make the effort to spend time with them as I realise the importance of sustaining positive relationships.

Social activities at a football club are not only limited to happy occasions with family and friends. They can also take the form of welfare programs, volunteer community involvement, ongoing education sessions, religious groups and mentoring. Club social activities away from competition are essential for balance; focussing on just football is a recipe for disaster. Stress so often accumulates and if it finds no release it can lead to fragmentation and poor performance on many levels—whether it's by physically affecting your immune system, psychologically leading to depression or negatively influencing your relationships.

Spiritual

Each individual's perspective on spirituality can vary greatly. Many see spirituality as an individual's religious values and beliefs. In the sporting sense, though, it can be thought of somewhat differently. Here spirituality refers to the individual developing the ability to view themselves on a deeper level—a level very different to the way athletes have traditionally been viewed. This, in turn, can also allow the athlete to view his teammates less superficially. Many sporting teams display a strong essence of spirituality without recognising it or valuing it. Spirituality can be responsible for positively changing the dynamics within a team and it can come in many manifestations.

In a team sport the most important thing is to think of oneself as being part of a team: not as an individual but as a link in a chain—a chain that must remain linked in order for it to succeed. If players think of themselves as individuals, success can't be achieved. Each player must love being a part of the team and genuinely love their team members. This thought is traditionally uncharacteristic of a male-dominated sporting code such as Australian Rules football, but once a player genuinely loves and cares for his teammates, he becomes less self-centred. When he pauses and reflects on what he can do to help his teammate, the focus is taken off him as an individual and the quest for success has commenced. If all team members think about helping their teammates become better players—and if they do so genuinely, for they *must* be genuine—a structure is created that can sustain their faith in themselves and each other throughout the most difficult of challenges.

Harry O'Brien—Being part of a team

Coming to the realisation that you can make your teammate a better player is what it's all about. Helping others definitely helped me—not just in sport, but in life.

Chris Dawes—Perspective on the team

One of our strengths is that there are no cliques in the club. We are all connected and respect each other. More importantly, we enjoy each other's company.

Dane Swan, who is the most rotated player in the AFL and who has the highest disposal statistics in the league, repeatedly comes off the ground to be rotated so that his teammates can be given an opportunity to go on. Historically, players of his level of expertise remain on the ground for longer, striving to get more disposals, more goals and more success. Dane strives for collective achievement and this selflessness has achieved him notoriety. In 2010 he won the AFL Players' Association's Most Valuable Player award, surprisingly by coming off the ground more often. Such selflessness was an important contribution to the team's overall performance.

Player rotations at Collingwood are generally based on scientific formulas and methodologies, but at times it's more effective for the players themselves to determine when it's their turn to leave the ground and give a teammate his run. Occasionally, when under pressure, they have forgotten this and so have lost an opportunity to claim a win. But when, upon reflection, they began to think of the team again, they once more became a formidable force.

Mick often repeats a very profound phrase, 'Great people are those who make others better.' This corresponds with the view that to help yourself, you need to help others. Still thinking of others, Dane donated his prize of a car for winning the Most Valuable Player award to a charity, the N.I.C.K. Foundation, which, like Dane, strives to help others become great.

Paul Licuria, who was Collingwood's player development and VFL manager, typifies these qualities. His impressive football achievements include winning the Collingwood best and fairest trophy on two occasions and playing nearly 200 games of league football. Even more impressive is his ability to genuinely give to others. This he has done as a player and as a staff member. He has frequently assisted the Salvation Army—often on several nights in a single week—to help the homeless. His tireless efforts to help charities, his community involvement and his great empathy and assistance for teammates who have lost their way come naturally to Paul.

Paul Licuria—Life's lessons

The best thing I've got out of footy is the relationships with the wonderful people I've met along the way. What is so unique about it is working together to achieve the ultimate success.

Acts like Paul's unites a group and causes others to emulate him. Once the athlete—or any person, for that matter—can step off the road to self-indulgence and give a hand to someone else in need, they are bound to develop as a person. When a person offers their hand to someone in need, they have demonstrated the greatest love. This is one way of defining spirituality.

David—The South African altitude training camp

Seeing people in need has been no more evident in my life than on a visit to South Africa. In 2007 I travelled with the Collingwood Football Club to Potchefstroom in the former Transvaal Republic, only 120 kilometres from Johannesburg, for an altitude training camp.

As the camp progressed, the players were forced to entertain themselves as the accommodation didn't include all the luxuries of home. A lack of infrastructure in the town meant that the power would go off for two to three hours a day. Meanwhile, the usual suspects in the football group would fraternise and play cards. These games were often for money and played under the thatched roofs in the warm summer afternoons, after our strenuous training sessions had been conducted.

The camp provided a wonderful opportunity for us all to see life from a different perspective and to build a greater appreciation of what opportunities we had back in Australia. Living for a short time in Potchefstroom meant being exposed to the living conditions in the local shantytowns. It was appalling to walk through these communities and feel their hopelessness. The whole party felt uncomfortable; we were voyeurs looking on in disbelief. Each one of us was thinking back to our life in Australia and could only feel a sense of having won Tattslotto when reflecting on our own lives. To have access to clean clothes, a house, healthy food, education and good jobs were luxuries in comparison to the squalor in which these people were forced to live. We felt remorse and empathy. It made sense of the players' need for the escapism of the card games.

In the latter part of the training camp, a party of about 20 players and staff were offered the opportunity to go on a tour of Soweto, an outer suburb of Johannesburg comprising some of the poorest townships of the city. Not all of the group attended. Mick stayed behind and Geoff Walsh and I led the party. While we were getting organised to head off, Alan Didak approached me and handed me something; it was a bundle of money the size of a 600 ml water bottle. It was all the money he had won from the poker games they had been playing. Alan told me to find someone who I really believed needed it and to give it to them. I asked him why he wouldn't come along and give it to someone himself and he explained that he would find it too difficult. 'Just do it for me mate!' he urged and pressed me to promise not to tell anyone.

Our little tour group headed off and one of the places we visited was an orphanage. Here we saw children who had been left without parents for many reasons, but mostly due to AIDS. The matron and her staff worked there under very difficult conditions, not dissimilar to the places our football group was seeing on a daily basis. The players, the other staff and I were nursing babies and playing with children who knew no other life. They simply looked on their visitors as a novelty and some welcome entertainment in their otherwise monotonous lives.

It's difficult to see suffering of any kind, but there's something about children suffering that touches you at the very core. How could we help these children? What could we do to ease their lives a little? Players and staff simply gave what they had. We reached deep into our pockets and gave whatever money we were carrying. Some of our group took the shirts off their backs, took off their caps and handed them to children and looked around for what else we had that we could give.

I took the matron aside and gave her the wad of money from Alan. I told her to use the money as she saw fit to help these young children. Her face was one of disbelief and her eyes welled with tears. She looked at the money I was handing her with absolute shock— it was as if she had never seen such a vast amount of money before, let alone been given it. She extended her gratitude and embraced me, and I was torn. I wanted to keep Alan's promise of not letting on where the money came from, and yet I so keenly wished to inform her of the generosity of this young man.

Alan didn't do this to cleanse his soul or por- tray himself as a spiritual hero. Being anonymous, it was a genuine act of kindness. When I handed over the money, I realised I was actually handing her much more—I was handing her hope. It left me feeling numb but showed me how one act of grace can instantly lift your hopes for mankind. Alan has received such negative press from people who don't even know him.

David—Knowing yourself

Back in 2000, I went on my first altitude training camp with the Australian swimming team. Many world-class swimmers of notoriety had been there before. I was sharing a room with Chris Fydler. Chris was not as well known as some of the other ath- letes, but sharing a room with him for several weeks gave me an insight into and an appreciation of an athlete who really knew himself.

Chris was happily married with a young family and valued them very highly. As well as his involvement in swimming, he was a lawyer working with PriceWaterhouse Coopers. He was a 100-metre freestyler who had represented Australia at two previous Olympic Games—in Barcelona and Atlanta—and over his career had been the Australian swimming captain for four years. Unfortunately, at the previous games he had fallen short of an Olympic medal and this was his aim for the fast-approaching Sydney Olympics.

As everyone knows, to be an Olympic athlete you must have dedication and a strong work ethic. But sometimes there's a tiny difference between one athlete and another in their pursuit of success and that can really make a huge difference. One of the differences I noticed with Chris was that he had an intuitiveness that enhanced his performance. He sensed if there was a need to monitor his training load or his physiological responses. He left no stone unturned in his pursuit to understand this feeling that something was not right or needed attention.

Because of this intuitiveness, Chris sought answers and was able to respond to them appropriately. This could mean he would be up at 5 a.m. to have his blood levels measured and make sure he was regularly monitored. Unlike many athletes, though, he would seek the results promptly. He did this to closely monitor his physical wellbeing in order to avoid being overtrained in the altitude conditions. Based on these results and his discussions with his coach, his day could comprise two gruelling sessions in the pool, extra weights training and cross-training to improve his performance. All this as a result of his own inquisitiveness and ability to sense the need for investigation and feedback.

What I found was most significant with Chris was his understanding of himself. He recognised and was able to admit his own capabilities and limitations. He would continually ask questions until he was satisfied that his intuitions were answered or confirmed. He was realistic and was able to recognise that he was not going to win a medal in the 100-metre men's freestyle. So he focussed on the relay team, a place where he believed he was better suited. He had a process and knew his capabilities.

While on the camp, I noticed that although he would listen to new ideas and innovations, he never accepted fads. Chris worked on building a training process based on proven research or principles. Because of this, he stuck to the process even when he felt he was not improving at the rate he had hoped he might. He trusted his coach and never complained or blamed others when things weren't going his way. Therefore, he did not compromise his training but continued to believe in himself, his program and his coach.

I remember the discussions Chris would have with his Sydney coach, the innovative Brian Sutton; I was impressed with their relationship. Such genuine respect for one another—Brian making feasible suggestions or recommendations with the view to manipulating his training and loading and Chris knowing himself so well that he was able to recognise whether this was the direction he should go or not. He had the ability to negotiate this with

Brian; the communication was always open. Chris lived in the present but maintained his focus. He was honest in his assessment of himself and could articulate this, and he knew how to get the best out of himself—a quality that, unfortunately, is not always apparent in all elite sportspeople.

History tells us that the Australian 4 x 100-metre men's relay team, made up of Chris Fydler, Michael Klim, Ian Thorpe and Ashley Callus, won the gold medal at the 2000 games. They beat the formidable US team against the odds in one of the most exciting events of the Sydney Olympics. The world looked on in shock as the unexpected happened. This win lifted the whole swimming team and they recorded the most medals won to date.

At the conclusion of any sporting event or competition, athletes are able to reflect back on their performance, sometimes with pride, sometimes with regret or sometimes blaming someone else. Chris can look back on his career and know that he achieved the ultimate success for a swimmer, an Olympic gold medal in his own country. But more importantly he can look back and know that, medal or no medal, he went into the event with an honest self-assessment, and as a man who knew himself.

Success is about knowing oneself. For when someone does this, they can listen to people's opinions and be able to objectively assess whether there is any merit in it. They can take criticism without offense and work towards becoming better. But by far the most important quality required in knowing oneself is honesty.

Michael Klim—On Chris Fydler

Chris and I were rivals and we were competing for the 100-metre freestyle spot. He was extremely professional and he was quite clever in utilising all of his resources to get the best out of himself. He didn't over-analyse, he kept it simple and he was very realistic about his ability. He trained specifically to meet his needs.

The superior man blames himself. The inferior man blames others.

NFL coach Don Shula

Taking responsibility

When an athlete is able to be honest in their self-assessment, they recognise that they must also take responsibility. Take an athlete who has had ongoing weight issues. Developing a good constitution takes effort and time and relies on a balanced approach to life. It is by consistently adhering to this that positive outcomes are realised.

Equally, balancing energy expenditure and energy input sustains a balanced physiological function. When there is a significant increase in either one of these two areas—input or output—one becomes dominant, just like a seesaw overloaded at one end. If an athlete is eating more calories than they are burning, they will gain weight, and if they burn more calories than they eat, the reverse will occur. This is often due to an inconsistency in behaviour, which can lead to undisciplined habits with negative results.

What an athlete consumes is a decision that they have made. The one who eats low-fat foods in reasonable portions will lose weight and the one who makes poor food choices will not. Controlling the input and output enables the body to adapt to that stimulus. Unnecessary increases in the body fat of an athlete will have crucial impacts on their performance. It can affect their endurance, running efficiency and power output. Conversely, a younger player may need to gain weight and achieve greater muscle mass to compete with opponents with more strength and power.

Ben Reid, who was recruited to Collingwood in 2007, arrived as a skinny, 78-kilogram, 195-centimetre kid. He currently plays at 99 kilograms with greater power and strength. The model that was applied required specific, prescribed planning that incorporated intensified weight training, regular food intake, supplementation, reduced aerobic training sessions and close monitoring. Ben's compliancy and commitment to meet the nutritional plan showed his dedication and sense of responsibility.

To initiate the quantum leap for a balanced life takes desire, commitment and self-management—subtle changes that need to be sustained for the end goal to be achieved. Many players are prepared to change their behaviour but need support along the way. The philosophical approach applied at Collingwood is built around an empowerment that enables the player to *embrace* the shift—not only in their food intake but in all their behaviours. Ultimately, it's the player's acceptance of change that enhances him both as a person and an athlete—as the old saying goes, you can lead a horse to water but you can't make it drink.

Once a person takes responsibility for their own actions and becomes committed to the intervention, positive change will occur. If an athlete is being dictated to and forced to comply, it's more likely that their commitment to the goal will wane. For example, a player who has had difficulty maintaining a specific body weight and is continually punished for not meeting his goals will be less likely to create that vital shift. Ownership needs to be established and responsibly accepted.

Balance

Harry O'Brien—Life balance

You have a limited amount of energy as a human being. If you just put it into football, you can miss out on the other wonderful, fulfilling things in life that football can't provide.

The most successful of all athletes are those who can maintain balance. Balance in their training, in their personal lives and in their place in the world. Balance is a vital key and everyone's balance differs. Most athletes have, at some stage, lost their balance and gone off the tram tracks. It's important for them to understand why this has happened so that a repeat fall in that area is less likely.

Our greatest glory is not in ever falling, but in rising every time we fall.

Confucius

Alan Didak—Balance

When I first came over to the Collingwood Football Club, life was all about footy to me. But after a few hiccups in life you realise who your real friends are. I had to make a few choices. Initially, I found it difficult because there was no balance in my life. Now, when I'm away from footy, I love being with my partner, family and friends. It's not all footy for me now. I'm so lucky to have a lot of good people around me. Life is not always going to be rosy, but spending life with the people I love gives my life balance.

The program at Collingwood has been so successful because it allows each individual to drive his own tram, even though, occasionally, they do go off the tracks. Identifying the key factors in your life helps you to achieve balance with momentum; it's extremely difficult to achieve this by yourself.

Man always travels along precipices. His truest obligation is to keep his balance.

Pope John Paul II

CHAPTER 5

LEADERSHIP

Effective leaders have an energy that elevates others to higher levels of self-belief. They possess qualities of self-awareness, intellect, vision, conviction and competency and use their power when necessary to achieve their objectives.

David—On Wayne Carey

In the early preseason of 1996 the Kangaroos played in a practice match in country Victoria. At the end of the game the players wandered into the rooms, happy with their win. Like many change rooms, there were supporters waiting outside who were equally happy with their team's performance. Among these supporters I noticed a young Kangaroos fan watching his heroes entering the rooms. This young boy had a severe respiratory disease; he had an oxygen tank by his side and a mask over his mouth to assist with his breathing. I thought he looked particularly frail.

As the players entered the change rooms their captain at the time, Wayne Carey, noticed this boy. He stopped and picked him up and carried him into the change rooms and his parents followed. Wayne helped the young fan move into the circle of players waiting for their captain to sing their theme song. He walked into the middle and held the boy up. He turned to his players and said, 'Now let's sing the song!' He began the Kangaroos' song with the boy held high in his arms.

This young fan's face had a smile from ear to ear. He was elated, not only with being in the room with his heroes, but because he had been singled out to come into the inner sanctum and then into the middle of the circle to experience what it felt like to be a part of his beloved team. To top this off he was being held by the man who, at the time, was known as 'the King'. The parents watched with tears welling up in their eyes at seeing their boy so consumed with excitement and so distant from his ailments.

It got me thinking about Wayne. It was only a few weeks after an incident involving a woman had led to a lot of negative and damming media attention. Yet here he was, with no cameras to catch this humane and sensitive act, an act that would have touched the very heart of this boy and been etched in his memory for the rest of his life—however long or short a time that would be. Not just the boy, but also his parents and the Roos' staff and players witnessed this moment of a leader being so positively influential. I remember the coach, Denis Pagan, saying, 'Where are the cameras and media now? This is what they should be reporting.'

I have thought a lot about Wayne as a leader. He has found himself in some unfortunate situations that have tainted his life forever. Yet this kind gesture with this young boy was one of many I witnessed from Wayne over the years, some with my own children. Although I don't condone his actions that drew the negative press, I still see Wayne Carey as a leader. As a captain he was able to lead a team on many occasions to a win, as well as being able to lead by bringing other players into the game. On this occasion I also saw an empathy that is not always present in elite athletes. He demonstrated to his fellow teammates that not only was he a courageous leader and player on the field, but he was also an empathetic one off it. In my view it was great leadership to give such hope to a small boy whose future was not looking so bright.

Wayne Carey—On leadership
Leadership is to encourage and inspire others. It's to make important decisive decisions. It is to relate to people and not make people feel less than. It is a position that you don't need a title for.

People often question whether leadership is innate or nurtured. You can watch a group of preschoolers and identify some children who are persuasive and influential on others and some who are followers. It would be interesting to observe if these children continue to possess the same traits as they grow older.

As children move from the playground to the sporting arena or the business world, leaders and followers can still be found. Sometimes though, people who hold positions of power are not capable leaders. It's common to find people in leadership positions who lack the strategic vision and motivation to energise others around them.

At times a leader's moral code can be questioned—this can often be to the detriment of the people under them. But the ones who create positive change and influence others for the good of all are the ones who not only possess the qualities listed above, but who also combine these with honesty and empathy. Those who can inspire others to become better are the genuine leaders; such leaders are often oblivious to the theories of leadership—for them, focussing on improvement in others comes naturally.

Have you ever walked into a workplace and felt a particularly positive energy? Not too often, perhaps. You can often feel it in schools where young children are engaged in valuable working teams. The energy in a workplace is the barometer of whether it has quality leadership. Usually there is that initial feel when you walk into a place. You sense a feeling of excitement and a buzz—this is commonly related to effective leadership. When you walk into a place and the energy levels are dull, the leadership is likely to be weak. Leadership is about harnessing the energy in others to garner commitment towards the group vision.

Keep away from people who try to belittle your ambitions. Small people always do that, but the really great make you feel that you, too, can become great.

Mark Twain

Leading by example

Mick—Caving at Mole Creek

Each season we take our first-year players away on camp for some mutual bonding that includes testing them mentally and physically.

On our first trip to Tasmania, though, we took the leadership group. Among them were Nathan Buckley, James Clement and Anthony Rocca, all ready for a trip consisting of mountain-climbing, trekking and caving. Our destination was Cradle Mountain in the Cradle Mountain–Lake St Clair National Park, but first we stopped off at the Great Western Tiers and a place called Mole Creek.

Here there was a three-chambered cave system, where the water disappeared into a mound before reappearing again. The person in charge of the tour was dubbed 'the Cave Woman'. She was a particularly petite female whose figure enabled her to fit into any small tunnel or chamber.

She pointed to a small hole in the base of the hill—barely wider than my shoulders (so small, it turned out, that Rocca had to enter the cave system through another, larger opening). She explained that we were to wriggle our way through this rocky burrow until we came to an opening where we would descend into a cave on the other side of the wall. We were given Hard Yakka suits and shoes and miners' hats with lights attached.

The only reason I trusted her was the fact she was still alive!

My journey began poorly when the light was knocked off my helmet, leaving me with just touch and sound to rely on. It was a short but extraordinary event. Coming out of the tunnel at the exit I saw a handful of quietly distressed men, relieved to have made it through. I felt the same way.

Years later, David and I brought a camp of eight first-years back to Mole Creek. There was a new and smaller tunnel to negotiate this time and while crouching down in the grotto to listen to our instructions I started to panic. My heart raced, I had clammy hands and I felt real dread.

We were told to breathe out before we entered the tunnel, because if our lungs were full of air it would be virtually impossible to fit through. The Cave Woman assured us we would make the distance before needing to breathe in and that we could do so upon exiting.

It brought back memories from my childhood in Ballarat, where my mates and I regularly ventured in and around mine shafts with total disregard for any possible consequences.

However, in this moment—as a husband and father—all I could think of was the consequence of something going wrong. What happens if there's an earth tremor and the surrounding rocks collapse in on us? What if I need to breathe in and get stuck? What if the person in front of me stops moving, blocking my exit? All of the possible negative scenarios of such a risky exercise were magnified in my mind and all I wanted to do was get as far from those caves as possible. But I couldn't and I didn't.

We all completed the task, wriggling through the cold, damp and dark passageway on our stomachs, arms stretched out in front, feeling for the feet of the person ahead. For me it was totally un-enjoyable and I felt great fear for most of it—but I did it.

At dinner that night we were chatting about families, football and life and I asked the boys, 'What has been your favourite experience on this camp?' There was a range of responses, including the moment on the Cradle Mountain climb when the mist cleared to reveal a fearful drop, the walk around Crater Lake and the visit to the Devil's Gullet. No one mentioned the Mole Creek tunnels.

I asked, 'What about the caving?' Without hesitation the general answer to this question was a resounding 'no'. They hadn't enjoyed the caving at all. 'Then why did you do it?' I asked. 'Because you did,' was the mass reply.

I had been coaching at an elite level for many years up to this point and yet you could have knocked me down with a feather at that response. It was a valuable lesson in leadership—perhaps one of the most significant lessons I have ever learnt. How could I have gone back to Melbourne asking these young men to do what I hadn't done myself? By doing it I had unwittingly led by example.

Sometimes as a leader you have an obligation to say, 'Do as you're told' and other times say, 'Do as I have.' It dawned on me that night at that dinner table that leadership means not just *guiding* as a leader, but *performing* as a leader.

Leadership can be taken for granted if you're not aware of your true effect on your troops. Responsibility comes at a price.

When we discussed our options recently for the upcoming first-year camp, which included Mt

Cook in New Zealand, north-west Tasmania and Mt Kosciuszko, I pushed very hard to climb Mount Kosciuszko instead of wriggling through a narrow rocky tunnel in the underground of our most southern state!

He regards his troops as his children and they will go with him into the deepest ravine. He regards them as his loved ones and they will stand by him unto death.

Sun-Tzu, *The Art of War*

In elite sport, athletes and coaches are often the focus of criticism by the media and the public. This can have an effect on performance. Assumptions are often made about high-profile sportsmen and women; they're expected to be role models in the community. People often assume that because a sportsperson is a leader in their field, they are a leader in all aspects of their lives—that they possess qualities of honesty and integrity simply because they hold a position of authority in the sporting arena. Unfortunately, scandals and rumours outside of their area of expertise—often in their personal life—can muddy the waters. Nick Riewoldt, the St Kilda captain, found himself embroiled in a scandal, accompanied by intense public scrutiny, which challenged his leadership. Though the law says you're innocent until proven guilty, media scrutiny can be damning.

Sporting clubs recognise the damage this kind of event can cause and work very hard to educate their athletes. At Collingwood, a leadership group is democratically formed and selected. This group helps to support the other players and uphold the ethos of the club. They uphold the values as well as drive the team. These players demonstrate what leadership is to the younger men coming into the sporting world and the public eye for the first time.

So many leaders in history have been accused of dishonesty—for example, Presidents Nixon and Clinton. In order to be seen and valued as an honest leader, a concerted effort is needed to display honesty and integrity in all aspects of life. Society's perception of honesty among leaders has become sceptical—the media encourages us to think that even if a person hasn't been found guilty, perhaps it's just because they haven't been caught yet.

This can be tough pressure for young athletes of 18 years who are just making their way in their new career path. To be suddenly thrust into an adult world under the watchful scrutiny of the media and public is difficult. It's no wonder that some stumble while trying to find their feet; after all, they're only human and everyone makes mistakes.

Even at a young age, though, true leaders take responsibility for their mistakes. When they deny responsibility for their wrongdoings, their dishonesty is magnified. Failures along the way are inevitable and acknowledging them takes courage, but it instils honesty, trust and respect from those around you.

Some people will never be leaders—that's true—but they can still work towards trying to attain some of the attributes that leaders possess. Most professional sporting clubs are devoted to developing their athletes off the field as well as on it. Sometimes scandals concerning sporting icons can't be avoided by the club, no matter how much effort or education they put into their employees, because in the end it's the employees' responsibility to live up to the club's standards. You can't make strawberry jam out of rusty nails.

People in positions of leadership are expected to have some level of competency. You could expect the Cave Woman at Mole Creek to have a sound knowledge of all the caves before conducting her tours.

Nick Maxwell, the current captain of Collingwood, has demonstrated competency as a footballer. He can negate key forwards, read the game exceptionally well and rebound swiftly into his team's offensive area. Nick also works to understand game structures, his teammates' capabilities and his opponents' strengths and weaknesses as well as directing his remaining defenders. This, combined with a strong vision for the future and a sound plan, gives legitimacy and respect to his leadership. It would be difficult to expect his team to follow his instructions if he did not show a significant level of competency and vision.

Nick Maxwell—On leadership

Being captain, I can't afford to have an ego. I believe you have to have an awareness of your players. I need to know what makes them tick. I'm here in this role to help them to get better and to help the team. I delegate, but I empower. I try to give the players confidence so that they can make the right decisions.

I seek opinions from the people I value, then I formulate the final decision. I try to understand what everyone's role is and respect it. Then I try to put myself in their position. I avoid making a decision straightaway. I seek opinions from the people I value, and then I make my final decision.

Using what you learn

Another quality successful leaders possess is an ability to use what they've learnt. Although some people appear naturally gifted and quick on the uptake, most of us can develop an in-depth knowledge in any field simply by investing a reasonable amount of time into study and research. Knowledge can be developed with a commitment to continual formal and informal learning.

The current North Melbourne coach, Brad Scott, is one such leader. He did not acquire the position of head coach at such a young age by chance. Brad's commitment to broaden his knowledge of coaching, sports science and the ever-changing game was a key reason for his selection as a senior coach. Many people noticed this in Brad during his short tenure as an assistant coach at Collingwood.

Brad Scott

Continual improvement is the key to coaching. You cannot rely simply on the things you learnt as a player and transfer them into your coaching and expect to be successful. The modern-day coach must constantly seek to improve through further study, self-examination and reflection. Science, technology and the game itself move at a rapid rate, and you have to make sure you are ahead of that curve otherwise you will get left behind. You can never stop trying to find a better way.

Inspiring

The leadership characteristics mentioned above can be enhanced by another quality: inspiration. As a leader in a football club, being inspiring means telling the players that they are capable of winning a Premiership and then detailing a process for the team to follow to do this. Guy McKenna, current coach of the Gold Coast Suns, often asked the players while he was an assistant coach at Collingwood, 'Do you want to drink alcohol while you're playing football? If you do, you might as well go back to your local club. Wait until you retire from playing in the AFL.' Winning a Premiership is the ultimate in football, he would tell them, recalling his own AFL Premierships while playing with the West Coast Eagles. McKenna has a unique charisma and an ability to motivate people by telling his stories, which leave an inspirational imprint.

Leaders unexpectedly find themselves in situations where they must perform; it's hard to be prepared for every situation. Collingwood President Eddie McGuire found himself in such a situation on the day of the drawn grand final in 2010. As mentioned earlier, both teams had assumed that that at the end of the day one team would go home victorious and one defeated. Eddie was no different to the rest, but he demonstrated leadership qualities when he gave his address to the team, coaches, staff and families at the dinner later that evening.

Eddie, no doubt, would have prepared a victory speech and a runner-up's speech. But it's unlikely that he had a drawn speech prepared. Despite a lack of preparation for the situation, he led with a motivating speech, giving praise where it was due and encouragement to go forward and face the day again with confidence. He referred to the idea that it was only half time, saying that the players and the club would go out and do it all again with a greater desire to win. He placed his full faith in them and gave them his trust and support. In a similar situation, many other leaders could have berated their team, shown their disappointment or even their anger—particularly when the team had gone into the game as the clear favourite.

Former American president John F Kennedy has been recognised as one of the greatest leaders of the modern era. Kennedy realised the enormous power that came with his position and hence the responsibility. He was applauded for his steady leadership during tumultuous times, particularly throughout the Cuban missile crisis in 1962. Kennedy kept his cool and gathered all the relevant background information. His timing and decision-making were crucial in preventing a third world war. He didn't shirk from his responsibilities; he faced them front-on.

Effective leaders are decisive. They need to act in the interests of the group, not just of particular individuals, and be strong—particularly in times of crisis. From an AFL perspective, the former could be related to recruiting or dismissing a player for the betterment of the club. Or it could be an instantaneous decision during a game to move a player to another opponent that could radically influence the outcome. Once the decision has been made the deliberation should stop. From that point on there is no going back and so the leader and his troops must support it 100 per cent.

Paul Licuria—Season of 2010
Watching players and key staff work under pressure and seeing them in the moment has been so influential on people. They were decisive and did not allow any distractions to interfere with their focus.

Of course, leaders may not win a popularity award for certain decisions, but a good leader looks beyond what people will think and considers only what is for the betterment of all, not just an individual. Making decisions isn't about making everyone happy. You'd question the suitability of a leader who was worried about being popular in times of decision-making. It can be lonely at the top!

Mick—Retirements

There is no right or wrong time to retire. There is no magical retirement age for an AFL footballer—certainly not 30 (as some may suggest). Just look at Craig Bradley (Carlton, 375 games), who played to the age of 38, and Kevin Bartlett (Richmond, 403 games), who didn't leave the game until he was 36. Both were wonderful players whose bodies and playing style allowed them to continue well beyond the age when most others stop.

Then there are players who retire early—usually forced to the sidelines permanently by injury. Dean Kemp, Don Pyke and Brett Heady from the West Coast Eagles all had to hang up their boots prematurely when their bodies failed them.

As a coach, you need to know when the time is right to give a player a nudge towards retirement.

It's no secret; I was very close to Paul Licuria when he was a Collingwood player. That made it all the more difficult when I had to have 'the' conversation with him in 2007.

Paul was never all that quick. Two knee reconstructions had caught up with him by the end of his career, reducing his speed even further. He couldn't get to contests—contests the team needed him to get to. He was going to ground too often. He wasn't the shut-down player he had once been.

Someone had to deliver the news; as his coach, that someone was me. There was no room for manoeuvring. I couldn't provide him with hope. I had to be firm, which may initially have been perceived as callous, but the correct move was made in the end.

Paul was deeply hurt when I suggested he retire and listed the reasons. It also hurt me to tell him the harsh truth. I told him he would more than likely play only in the VFL the following season with little chance of senior selection. For him, I said, this would be a disaster. After a 192-game career, in which his incredible work rate and consistency in the midfield earned him two Copeland Trophies (2001 and 2002), he wouldn't want to be seen as a 'hanger on', a possible target for ridicule. I told him he should be remembered for his hard work and dedicated contribution to Collingwood and to the game of Australian Rules football.

He took my news on the chin, though, as I knew he would. Once he went away and thought about his options he could see it was the right call. At the end of that season he retired.

Paul remained at the club in a VFL/AFL administrative capacity and mentoring role for a while. His great character, experience and football skills all provided invaluable assistance to the young Magpie, players.

For him, retirement came earlier than expected. As difficult as it was to push him in that direction after coaching him for eight years, I'm glad I was able to judge when his time was up and save his football reputation.

Nathan Buckley was another player that needed a little coaxing into retirement. As a Brownlow Medallist (2003), multiple Copeland Trophy winner, seven-time All Australian team member and Collingwood Team of the Century inductee, there's absolutely no question his football talent was immense. He was a champion of the game. But even champions need to finish at some stage.

A hamstring operation had slowed Nathan down. He, too, was going to ground too often. The signs were there and although thousands of Collingwood supporters would have loved them to go ignored, as his coach I couldn't turn a blind eye.

Nathan is a very proud man and, like so many sports stars, he was having trouble letting go. There is a mentality that they will last forever. He could still kick with pinpoint accuracy, mark and tackle—his footy brain was as bright as ever. But at 35 years of age his body was no longer up to scratch.

He approached many people, including myself, looking for validation that he should continue for one more year. I wouldn't have been true to him, to myself nor to the club if I had agreed to the suggestion of another season.

It was no longer a question of whether he should retire; he had to retire. A champion like Nathan doesn't want to be remembered as a lesser-quality player. Had he continued for another year, battling injury and body fatigue, his status as a brilliant footballer and his tremendous eight-year reign as Collingwood's captain may well have been tarnished. He did not deserve that. He also retired at the end of 2007 and remains at the club today in a senior role.

Leaders sometimes have to be harsh. You have to play devil's advocate to paint the true picture for the person in question when he can't see it himself. Sometimes he will listen, sometimes he won't.

I was at Footscray when Doug Hawkins was nearing the end of his career. An ACL operation had affected his agility and speed. It got to a point that I had to drop him from the senior side. I had a discussion with him then about his future and the possibility of retirement.

Instead of retiring, Doug played on and eventually he left Footscray and went to Fitzroy for the 1995 season. Having left Footscray myself five years earlier, I viewed this as a mistake for Doug, one that would taint his reputation as a great Bulldog, a veteran of 329 games. I still believe he should have remained a one-team player and received the accolades associated with this.

In a different sport—cricket—Ricky Ponting stood down as captain of both the Australian Test team and the one-day side in March 2011. He said that it was solely his decision to relinquish the captaincy but continue playing.

My outside observation of the Australian Cricket Board's decision-making processes for retiring players is that it lacks decisiveness and that this lack of leadership hinders the development of cricketing youth for the country.

If Ricky Ponting hadn't made the decision to stand aside (as reported by the media), would anyone else have forced him to look at the situation? There's a saying that 'It's harder to get out of the Australian cricket side than it is to get in'. This is a poor reflection of the leadership at the top of Australian cricket.

When wicketkeeper Ian Healy's form dropped off in the late 1990s and Adam Gilchrist was in blistering form in the one-day arena, it seemed that Adam would have to continue to wait patiently for Healy to retire before being given the gloves for the Test team. In the AFL, if a player is performing poorly, someone who is in form replaces him almost immediately. So who is calling the shots in cricket? Is it the part-time selectors in a full-time job? Is it the coach who is outranked by the captain? Is it the captain who is a teammate of the much-maligned player? What is the hierarchal system of the ACB? From where I stand, it looks a bit like the tail wagging the dog.

Too often it seems like major cricketing decisions are being made by the playing group. To me, this is a very dangerous situation. It's an archaic system that has never been rectified (even after our world Test ranking dropped to five). For the future progress of the game, something needs to change at the highest level of Australian cricket.

When the time comes to consider retirement, an athlete must think through the reasons that they are hanging on. They should think about the integrity of bowing out with dignity. Likewise, when an athlete considers making a comeback from retirement they should think twice. What is their true motive for having another go? Is it financial? Are they chasing a dream?

In 2010–2011 we saw a wave of Australian swimmers return to the pool after a brief retirement. Geoff Huegill, Ian Thorpe and Michael Klim all decided to have a second shot at the top. Having already achieved success, though, why would they risk doing their reputation harm by having another crack? In sporting history, very few make it back successfully.

Nathan Buckley and Paul Licuria are two among many players that I have had the 'retirement conversation' with. They listened and weighed up their options before concluding themselves that it really was the right time to walk away. For this, they are remembered for all the right reasons.

David—Making the best decision for the group

On the first year that the club took a group of executives with the players to Arizona, Eddie McGuire, Collingwood's president, was in our party. All of the executives were invited to join the players' expeditions. As in previous years, included in our activities was a climb of Mt Humphreys—a challenging task to say the least!

Based on their levels of fitness, we allocated the executives and some of the less conditioned players and staff to the first group and sent them off an hour earlier. This group was led by Mick. Our objective was to get all players to climb the 15 kilometre or so mountain trail in under three hours. Mt Humphreys' peak is the maximum altitude in Arizona, being just under 4000 metres, so the benefits the players achieve from this climb at high-altitude exposure are significant, both physiologically and psychologically. In simple terms, there is no easy way up. So for non-elite athletes the climb is difficult; at an elite athlete's pace, it's gruelling. In between Mick's group and mine, there were several other smaller groups, all formed and positioned based on their physical capabilities.

Mick is notorious for setting a fierce pace. All the players know that a walk with him means they are in for a session. I was leading the group with the most capable athletes. We left an hour after Mick's group and our aim was to meet at the peak at a similar time.

As I was ascending Humphreys Trail, about 90 minutes from the top, I saw ahead of me a figure sitting on some rocks, head down. I thought a player might have rolled an ankle and been told to descend back down to the base.

As I got closer, I realised it was Eddie and wondered what he was doing sitting there by himself. As I approached I could tell that he was exhausted and had broken away from the group because of this. I could also tell that he was very annoyed that this had happened. I asked him what was up. He said that Mick and his group had decided to leave him there and push on without him. He explained that the other groups had also passed him in their pursuit to make the ascent.

Because he didn't look very well I measured his oxygen saturation levels and heart rate and realised that he was struggling with the altitude. I knew he wasn't happy about Mick leading the others on, but I also suspected that Mick had made the correct decision. Nevertheless, I was still concerned about Eddie's disposition and knew it would be a wonderful achievement collectively if he were able to make it to the top.

In my group were staff members Paul Licuria and Mick Dugina. I made a quick decision and chose the latter to assist Eddie with his climb because of his sports-science background. I pulled him to the side, knowing that he would follow my instructions to the letter, and said, 'Get Ed to the top! I don't care how long it takes you.' I told him that even if he had to carry him, Eddie had to get to there. I instructed Mick to monitor him at the appropriate times and gauge how he was coping, to ensure that safety measures were enforced. I urged him to keep Eddie distracted and push him as hard as he was capable, without taking risks.

Paul and I and the rest of our group continued on to the peak, where we met up with the other groups who had completed the ascent, including the coach and the first group, which Eddie had originally been a part of. I pulled Mick Malthouse aside and asked what had happened with Eddie. He said that Eddie had showed signs of fatigue in the first 30 minutes and so after an hour he had had done what I thought—Mick had had to make a choice between Eddie and the players.

The group that I was leading waited at the summit while the other groups began descending. Despite the freezing conditions and growing agitation, we hoped that Mick Dugina would get Eddie to the top. After 30 minutes, the players were beginning to express their desire to descend as they felt he was not going to make it. Paul and I encouraged them to wait a bit longer because we knew that if anyone could get Eddie up to the summit, Mick Dugina could.

After approximately 40 minutes, I thought I could see two small, dark figures ascending up the track through the snow. A few minutes later the rest of the group noticed them and realised Eddie was actually going to make it. As he was approaching the boys began to call out encouragement to Ed, spurring him on.

Finally the pair reached the top. Eddie was hugging everyone and giving high-fives. He was elated with his accomplishment and the boys shared his happiness. After ten minutes or so we began the descent and later that evening we were able to say that the whole party had successfully completed one of the hardest activities at altitude, the climbing of Humphreys Peak.

Although Eddie was elated with his achievement, there was obvious tension between the coach and the president, though I feel exhaustion played a part in this. The next day Mick applauded Eddie's effort in front of the whole group and after a good night's rest, Eddie could see that the coach was a man who could be counted on to lead his troops, even under extreme pressure. Mick's philosophy had been that the army does not stop for the loss of one soldier; the fight must go on. Eddie acknowledged that Mick had had a greater responsibility—to the whole team—and had had the courage to show leadership when it was required.

He had made the correct choice. The aim, as well as the priority of the expedition, was to get the team to the top. After all, the altitude camp was to improve the players, not the executives. But Eddie was not your regular executive. Mick had been forced to make the decision for the betterment of the group, even at the risk of leaving the club's president to fend for himself and become quite angry. Mick had shown leadership and courage, in spite of the fact that this could have jeopardised his relationship with someone who had a position of title and influence at the club. It could have been detrimental to his coaching position, as well as to future altitude camps.

Leadership is not limited to the people in key roles; it can be shown by others as well. Mick Dugina demonstrated leadership by patiently encouraging and assuring Eddie that he would make it and he showed commitment by staying with him through the whole process. Eddie McGuire acknowledged Mick's support in a column he wrote several days later for the *Sunday Herald Sun*.

> Dugina did something that many people may be in a position to do, but often don't. Instead of stepping around me, he stepped up to me. I was his boss, but at that stage of the game he pitied me, without making me feel pitiful. He knew I'd give everything to get back up, but just didn't know how to do it. He compassionately showed me. There was no 'rah-rah' or motivational talk; he knows I've heard it all. All he did was stand one step behind me and guide me up the steep, slippery mountain . . . Mick Dugina got me there. He didn't need to help me and wasn't sure if it was appropriate that he should. But he did. And I managed. I barely noticed the long trek down the mountain.
>
> 'Help to get over the hump', *Sunday Herald Sun*,
> 16 November 2008

Lasting effects

With leadership comes power—sometimes extreme power. But leadership can be quietly powerful, unassumedly leading people for a common cause. Mother Teresa and Mahatma Gandhi had significant numbers of followers, but neither sought the glory or the fame. Nor did either of them use force to lead their flock; they led by example. They had firm beliefs in a cause and pursued it with conviction. The strength of their personal convictions did not allow them to deviate from their ideals. They both had thousands of followers, some of whom still carry on their legacy today; the Missionaries of Charity was founded by Mother Teresa and the establishment of the independence of India through non-violent means owes a lot to Gandhi. Both worked self-lessly to improve the conditions of humanity.

Examples of leadership occur every day at a football club—sometimes unexpectedly and sometimes from the least expected! These examples may be far removed from those of Mother Teresa or Gandhi, but they still make a difference in people's lives. The people who perform these actions are unlikely to be as blemish-free as in other areas of their life as these two servants were, but in their own way they have led others to feel better about themselves and given hope. However small these actions may be, they can still be very powerful to those who are directly affected by them—just as there is no doubt that Wayne Carey's actions would have had a powerful and lasting effect on that young boy's life. As each wave of young players enters the fray, there's always the hope and potential that they will find the right path and develop into leaders themselves.

CHAPTER 6

COACHING AND MENTORING

Nowadays most young athletes are encouraged to adopt a mentor or a coach to help them improve their performance, nurture their skills and empower them. But are these helpers exclusive to the sporting world?

Coaches have been around as long as the human race itself. For as long as there have been people needing to acquire skills, there have been people with knowledge and experience willing to coach. Older and more skilled members of a community have always shared their expertise with the younger and less-skilled members. In sport, as long as organised team sports have been going, they've been linked to coaches, especially from the early twentieth century.

The concept of mentoring, on the other hand, is a more recent addition to the sporting scene. Mentoring, however, dates back some three thousand years to Greek mythology and Odysseus. Odysseus, who was setting out for Troy, entrusted his house and the education of his son to his friend Mentor. Odysseus directed Mentor to impart his knowledge and wisdom to his son, to be a 'father-like' advisor.

Coaching

In sport, a coach has become a necessity. Today it would be unthinkable for a team—even at a junior level—to not have someone called 'the coach'. Over the last century, coaching in sport has developed enormously and is now a highly specialised role. Experience as a sportsperson is often not enough to qualify you to take on a coaching position.

At an elite level, the fact that you always see the head coach alongside the captain holding up the just-won Premiership cup indicates the importance of the role. Further to this, teams now have specialised coaches for particular sections of their team. For example, in the AFL there are forward-line, midfield, backline and development coaches. There are also goal-kicking, ruck, tackling and strength and conditioning coaches. Teams look to these coaches for direction and instruction; in teams where there is more than one coach, athletes seek out a specific coach to help them in an area where they need to improve.

Both in sport and in life a coach can also be regarded as a teacher, for a coach is an instructor, a tutor and a trainer. The coach's role is to teach others to become more skilled in the area in which they themselves are skilled and have vast knowledge. In sport, it's their job to finely tune athletes to become exceptional at their skill or talent. Who better to teach a midfielder (such as Scott Pendlebury or Dane Swan) how to clear the ball from stoppages and create opportunities than Nathan Buckley, who was an exceptional midfielder in his time? He is able to instruct a midfielder because he was once in that position himself; he can see the pitfalls as well as the potential opportunities and thus improve the midfielder's game.

Coaching has great value if it addresses behaviour that needs to be changed, improved or removed, but—as with all teachers—coaches' methods may vary. Some methods of coaching deliver instructions using a command-and-control approach. The famous VFL/AFL coach Ron Barassi worked in this style and achieved success with multiple Premierships at different clubs.

Can you remember your first day of school? Your first football game, music lesson or even the first time you were taught how to ride a bike? If you can recall further, each of these activities required some form of coaching. There would have been someone there guiding you. Did these experiences involve a style that was nurturing and encouraging or were they threatening and off-putting? Each of us has had such positive and negative experiences at some stage in our lives, which have left lasting impressions for one reason or another.

We all learn through different kinds of experiences and coaches or teachers can deliver the same knowledge or skill using totally different styles and methodologies. If you can recollect any of those earlier experiences, it obviously had some effect on you as a learner—but was it positive or negative? Whichever it may be, it highlights how important the role of a coach is in sport and the effect they can have (or not have) in the development of the athlete.

Mick—Dictatorial methods

Football coaching is not democratic. All of the great coaches of the game have been dictatorial to a certain extent. This is because democracy is slow and cumbersome and requires too much dialogue with others. It takes time—time that you don't have in the coaching fast lane.

This is not to say that the processes of selection, training methods, recruitment, player welfare and the like are done by one person. These roles must be done by experts from many fields to get the right result.

But the ultimate decisions made on game structures and strategies and match-day scenarios come from one voice. During a match there's no room for a panel or a composite of coaches discussing moves. Coaches at AFL level have to live and die by their own methods. Some advice I received early on in my career from the late Allan Jeans (my St Kilda coach from 1972 to 1976) was to be Mick Malthouse and no one else. It was advice that he himself had been given by the legendary Norm Smith.

Sure, you will take into consideration guidelines and principles from other sources, but primarily you are an island. I have been described as a lone wolf and as such I will never blame anyone else for a loss or a bad season; it is by my hands only. By saying this, I don't mean to minimise the role of assistant coaches or others within the organisation; it's just that we all have a role to play. They, too, have a voice and ideas, but they must be delivered at the right time and someone has to take ultimate responsibility.

The coaches that I played under at St Kilda and Richmond all had very different styles of leading and various methods of coaching. Each one got the best out of me and allowed me to reach my full potential as a footballer.

Jeans was very much a 'do as I say' type of coach. He had experience, knowledge and the respect of his charges to be able to lead this way with effect. A great oral motivator, he often used inspirational speeches and stirring words to encourage his players.

I responded to this style as a young player in the '70s, however things have changed dramatically for the youth of today. Rarely do we use motivational tapes, films or lectures. Modern professional footballers rely heavily on their own preparation and pride. Instruction from their coach about strategy is more important today than ever before.

I greatly admired Jeans both as a coach and a person and I was deeply saddened by his passing in July 2011. The outpouring of emotion from his former players at this time was a true sign of his character and the profound effect he'd had on those he worked with. He changed the game and he will be missed by all.

When I moved to Richmond in 1976 I found Tommy Hafey had a softer approach. He would appeal to your emotional side and psyche by suggesting that 'you're letting the team down' if you didn't play to his expectations. He was very encouraging, though, and gave a pat on the back when it was deserved. He ran a strict physical regime that he also adhered to himself.

Tony Jewell made it 'his way or the highway'. He was direct and brutal, for good reason. The club had failed to deliver for a number of years. He put us through the hardest preseason I've ever encountered. Many players fell by the wayside, but those that remained were part of the great 1980 Richmond Premiership side.

These three coaches had ultimate success in football. Jeans coached four Premierships: one at St Kilda and three at Hawthorn. Hafey won four grand finals with the Tigers. And Jewell had the one Richmond Premiership.

I enjoyed playing for all of my coaches and still respect them greatly. They each helped formulate the type of game style I wanted to convey to my player groups. I've developed this further with my own personality and from adjusting to the times, taking things from other sports as well.

I hope the men I have led have enjoyed playing for me. My main desire, with all of the players I have coached, has been to make them more knowledgeable about the game, worldlier (by way of travel for training camps and international games) and better educated through academic study or by learning a trade. I hope this has helped them to become better players and better men.

Football coaching has many responsibilities; those responsibilities cannot be avoided, put off or delegated. They are part and parcel of the role; you have to accept that and then act upon it.

Harry O'Brien—Mentoring

It's all about empowerment. Great mentors can instil belief in you.

As suggested above, the preferred method of coaching is one that enables the athlete to sustain their success and improve through empowerment and nurturing. Being told how badly you are executing some skill or other is not likely to help you learn to do it better. However, if you're asked what you think the problem might be, have a discussion and then try a new method, eventually you will work out which is the best method and acquire the skill.

An AFL midfield player may be getting frustrated because he's not holding opponents who are breaking through stoppages. His coach may ask why he believes this is occurring. The player may not know or may recognise that he's lacking strength. The coach may acknowledge this and suggest a new program of strength and weight training, which is designed consultatively. In the meantime, the coach may also suggest a different tackling method, such as getting closer to the opponent instead of lunging before tackling. This could enable a greater grasp on opponents and thus increase tackling effectiveness. The player will work on developing his strength in the gym on his own, following a program he helped design, in conjunction with practising this new tackling technique. The player will no doubt feel some improvement over the weeks and will believe in the method because he has had some input in addressing his deficiency. In the discussion, the coach guided the player, but crucially also allowed the player to participate in the formulation and implementation of the solution.

This may seem like a simple example. But the coach could have spoken condescendingly or angrily to the player and dictated the method that the athlete should have used. The athlete may have followed this instruction and improved his technique or, discouraged, he may have lost confidence and become reluctant to make any changes to his program and technique.

A great coach will draw on an athlete's existing expertise to facilitate and accelerate learning and dramatically increase performance. Particularly positive results occur when the relationship between coach and athlete is based on mutual respect. Essentially, coaching is a highly personalised one-to-one development program. Coaching focuses on possibilities and potential, on *doing* things that facilitate learning, rather than just telling. Thus, athletes unlock their own potential and maximise performance by following through themselves.

Mick—On coaching

Collingwood defender Alan Toovey absorbed all information on his strengths and weaknesses. He improved on the latter through practice. By high-lighting both sides of his game we allowed him to see what areas needed to be worked on and also how to use his strengths to maximise his output. He left no stone unturned to arrest any areas of his game that would preclude him from a spot in the senior side. He is still very left-sided but he makes up for it with incredible determination.

Former Footscray captain Stephen Wallis needed positive reinforcement to deliver his best. He respected my opinion and took it on the chin when I delivered a negative assessment of some com-ponents of his skill set. (He lacked pace and didn't have a long kick.) However, I in turn respected his acknowledgement of his faults and provided posi-tive feedback on his capabilities. (He was hard as nails and had a wonderful ability to win the one-on-one ball.) He worked within his range of ability to become a very good footballer.

Nick Maxwell—On coaching

Great coaches know how to get the best out of each player. They know how to tweak them.

Coaching within the AFL is intense and it sometimes operates in a volatile working environment—particularly when games are locked in a tight arm-wrestle. High-performance coaching requires a high level of commitment, a stable coach–athlete relationship, a focus on medium- to long-term planning, established monitoring techniques, effective decision-making expertise and leadership skills to control performance variables.

In team sports, the challenge is to deliver the message to a variety of athletes with different learning styles. The specific challenge is getting the message across effectively to many people while allowing each athlete to have ownership of the message and relate it to their own play. With their coach as a guide, players need to learn how to generate their own questions, work through their deficiencies and correct their own behaviour. Ultimately, coaching is about helping the athlete to become self-evaluative, self-correcting and self-generating.

Mick—On coaching (continued)

David Hart had reached his limit in the West Coast forward line so I suggested a switch to the backline. By the end of his career he was an All Australian back pocket. Teaching him how to play this new role was a matter of physically challenging him to hone his skills. By walking him through the strategies step by step and then physically showing him how best to play the position, he was able to grasp the message and translate it into action. David learnt best by example.

Collingwood forward Chris Dawes, on the other hand, will grasp most things presented to him in print. He is highly intellectual, so for him practice goes hand-in-hand with theory. Therefore, to teach him new structures or strategies, the process is fairly simple—write it down, perhaps with a graphic to emphasise the point. Chris will then convert this philosophy into function at training as he physically practises what he has read.

Mick—On coaching (continued)

Paul Medhurst was a wonderfully gifted All Australian footballer. He had an accurate kick, he never lacked courage and he could lose an opponent in an instant with his mobility. Unfortunately Paul struggled with the concept that, at Collingwood, he had to fit into a role that was fairly foreign to his previous experience with the Fremantle Dockers. He failed to blend into our team structure. He still had the same abilities, but try as he may he could not gel with the concept of the whole and consequently lost his position in the side midway through our Premiership season (2010).

It's not unusual for athletes to reject a coach's accurate evaluation of their performance. At times they can't see their deficiencies and so immediate, honest, accurate feedback is needed from the coach. This is particularly crucial in the heat of the battle, for this allows for deficiencies to be addressed and adjusted when time is precious. At these times, succinct feedback is vital. For progress to take place, accurate self-evaluation needs to be done. Providing the right feedback or stimulus allows the athlete to acquire and develop a skill. Seeing the deficiency is one thing; knowing the type of stimulus you need to provide is another.

Mick—On coaching (continued)

Travis Cloke always had a super-long kick, though he lacked accuracy. The Collingwood big man was his own worst critic. He suffered constant media scrutiny and crowd harassment, made worse by his own self-doubt. We, as a match committee, however, had great faith in him as an individual and as a team member. We tried many different coaching techniques to help Travis' aim, because as a key forward, kicking goals is a must. He tried his heart out at an extraordinary work rate. We took great delight in his efforts. Our job was to keep reinforcing the positive with him. Eventually we had the idea for Travis to kick for goal repeatedly, from different angles and distances, wearing a headset playing crowd noise. He learnt to silence the racket in his ears and concentrate on hitting his target. His game and goal-kicking ability has improved dramatically over time and he's now a crucial member of the Magpie forward line.

It's quite common to see athletes who appear to have 'poor' execution or technique, but a very productive outcome. Dane Swan, who has won three Copeland Trophies at Collingwood, appears to have an awkward running style. His running technique has none of the efficiency of world 100-metre champion Usain Bolt, but his duck-like gait still enables an effective result throughout games. His sprint times and agility tests are superior at Collingwood. More importantly, they display a dynamic power throughout games. The question that is posed occasionally is: why doesn't Dane change his running gait? The response is that if it works efficiently and is not broken, why fix it? There are numerous other examples that demonstrate this, whether in swimming, golf, tennis or Australian Rules.

The technical components of Australian Rules football will continue to improve as resources and training methods develop. The tactical area, which is continually evolving set plays, game styles, game tempos and players' roles, is becoming more comprehensive. Players are required to grasp all these facets of the game and apply them to their performance. With the assistance of technology, improved coaches-to-player ratios and quality of educational delivery, an effective learning environment for the individual to develop into a better player has been provided. Effective coaching is about knowing when to intervene.

Mentoring

Mick has often stated that he is committed, more than anything else in his role as coach, to helping each of his players to develop as a whole person and not just as a player. His goal is that when they are finished at the club, they will come out as a better person.

Mick—On mentors

I left my home town of Wendouree West when I was 17 and moved to the St Kilda Football Club (each of the 12 VFL clubs had a country zone). My first VFL coach was Allan Jeans. What a wonderful leader to have for my opening attempt at football at the top level!

Jeans, a policeman at the time—football was a part-time job then—set very high standards for his charges and that left a positive lifelong impression on me. He was, at times, in your face and it was always apparent what he stood for. His strategies and game plans were very defensive, which suited me as a defender and has quite clearly fashioned my own coaching tactics. I learnt so much from him in the four and a half years I spent under his reign and consider myself lucky to have had one of the game's great coaches as my first VFL mentor.

When I moved to Richmond halfway through 1976, I took on a new mentor in the then Tigers' coach, Tommy Hafey. He was very different to Jeans in his on-field approach, in that his game plan was very offensive. The Hafey trademark style was to kick long into the forward line. Though this differed to my experience at the Saints, Hafey was the wonderful, caring person I needed at the time. He took a special interest in all of his team members. He frequently invited the players and their partners to dinner at home with his family. He also had the amazing habit of ringing each player on the Friday night prior to a match, which made you feel important and eager to do his faith in you justice. He instilled discipline in the club with a strict fitness regime, which he still continues today, swimming and working out on a daily basis as well as speaking in schools on healthy lifestyle choices. Although Hafey resigned at the end of my first season at Punt Road, he made an important impression on me.

In my early years my father suffered from illness and spent large amounts of time hospitalised. I was lucky, though, to have a gentleman and incredible grandfather (Timothy Canty) to look after me, staying in the background, but always there when I needed him. He inspired my love of the Australian bush. My father inspired me with his courage, which I will never forget. Both of these men shaped my life for the better—I could quite easily have headed towards trouble, but instead, I headed towards football.

I couldn't have had a better introduction into the VFL with Jeans and then Hafey as my coaches and mentors, though without my original football mentor, who kept me on track and allowed me to follow my dream of playing footy at the highest level, I wouldn't have made it to the VFL. My under-16 Ballarat North coach, Lyndsey Lyons, was a local policeman who took great interest not only in coaching the football team, but also in helping its members to develop into upstanding young men.

After convincing me to move to the football club (where many of my schoolmates from St Paul's Tech played) he immediately made me feel welcome. Looking back, I can see how he subtly influenced me for the better and kept me on the straight and narrow. He made me think about my responsibilities and gave me a chance in the sport that I loved. To him, I am so grateful for this.

As a coach myself, this is the kind of impression I have always wanted to make on the young players in my charge. When a young player first comes to an AFL club, more often than not they have just left home (some moving interstate and away from their families to fulfil their AFL dream). This means that guidance from their parents is no longer as prominent, which is where we, as leaders, need to fill the gap.

Young men don't always seek to be mentored. However, when an 18-year-old boy joins a football club and becomes our responsibility, then he needs to be mentored and mentored well.

Mick—On mentoring

The 2010 draft gave us 12 new players in their late teens and early twenties. Our senior squad makes an annual trip to Arizona for a training camp, which our draftees generally miss out on because they arrive at the club too late in the year. To compensate for this, David and I decided that the best course of action would be to have a mini training camp for the new boys each year. In January 2011 we went to Mt Kosciuszko and Thredbo. This was our first camp in New South Wales.

I have a strong belief in peer mentoring so, as usual, the player group of 12, David and development coach Craig McCrae and I sat around the lounge room to get to know each other. No questions have to be answered, the players can speak about anything they want and be questioned by their new teammates or myself. Over half of the group came from single-parent families, some due to death and others due to family break-up. In their stories that night they spoke of life and death, parents and grandparents, girl-friends and mates. A tragic event had occurred in the life of more than half the boys there. We had begun the evening sitting at arm's length apart from each other. By the end of the night, after we all spoke about our life experiences, we were arm in arm in a protec-tive manner. Clearly, player mentoring had started to develop from that night for this set of young men.

We must never forget that all players have strengths and weaknesses outside of football. We have been recruiting from Ireland, the United States and interstate for several years now. As much as these players feel they can stand alone, as the season wears on, many become desperately homesick. Home's just a phone call away, but the personal touch is paramount.

As family plays such a significant role in a young person's life, we never deny a player time spent with his loved ones—in fact, I encourage it. Parents are the first mentors of a young man and his siblings provide further love, understanding and support. By giving our players time off to spend at home, we are extending the role of the mentor and guardian and this can only have a positive effect on the individual.

Dane Swan seemed indifferent when he arrived at the club. I didn't know whether he was more committed to football or his mates, none of whom were part of our squad at the time. Upon early troubles in his career, I sat Dane down and said to him in no uncertain manner, 'Make a choice—AFL football or suburban football.' He had to make a decision and it would come at a high price. I said he had to move suburbs to draw a line between what he had and what we needed to have—a committed footballer whose focus was on the immediate demands of our game. Dane spoke to his parents and the decision was made. Football at AFL level meant too much. So he moved a significant distance from his home at the time. His parents were and continue to be great mentors; he just needed an extra shove from his football family.

The life of an elite footballer is not normal. And the demands on the young are far greater today than they were even 40 years ago. For a start, we rob these teenagers of their youth with a strict and demanding training and game schedule that also includes diet and psychology. We really do ask a lot of these young men. The scrutiny on them—their football perform-ance and their outside life—is twice as much (if not more) than any regular job would be.

The temptations of an alternative lifestyle—of fooling around with alcohol, drugs and perhaps even violence—are extraordinary. People willing to bring them down often target young men with high profiles and a good pay cheque. It takes great strength and character to ignore these offers and stay focussed on football as a *life* not just a job.

We can't be guardians 24 hours a day, although we can stay on our toes and be ready to provide assistance when it's needed and guidance when it's required.

While leading our boys to a more acceptable life—where they are responsible for all of their actions—I have also tried to give them an awareness of life outside of football in general. I want them to be worldlier and our annual team camps reflect this with much emphasis placed on learning about the culture of the countries and cities we travel to.

On our training camp to South Africa the boys visited many settlements, including Soweto, the likes of which they would have never seen before. Likewise, our accommodation in Arizona, in the small town of Flagstaff, provides an opportunity to sample the culture of this part of the United States.

I respect the absolute importance of education. Fortunately, the football club makes available many opportunities for our players to study. Brad Dick was illiterate when he began at Collingwood and he now knows how to read and write. James Clement achieved a double-degree at university while playing AFL football. These men should be proud of their academic accomplishments.

As a leader and as a coach, mentoring a young person is perhaps the most important role you will ever play. You must lead by example and think deeply about the direction and advice you are imparting to an individual. A supportive, understanding and caring mentor is just as vital as a disciplined and thorough coach.

Brad Dick—Development

Simon Lloyd introduced me to a reading and writing program. Before, I just used to look at the pictures in the newspaper. Now I can read! I'm currently reading a book about Lance Armstrong that was recommended to me by Tarkyn Lockyer.

Coaching is generally seen as developing the technical, tactical and physical qualities of an athlete. As stated earlier, coaching delivers particularly positive results when a relationship is established between coach and athlete based on mutual respect; this allows for the development of a relationship with personal growth.

Effective mentors communicate their belief that challenges can be overcome and greatness accomplished. But how is this done? Mentoring is all about successful relationships. While a coach knows that he must teach and impart skills or knowledge, using whatever method he selects, he is not necessarily concerned with relationships. He knows that his role is clearly defined and outcomes-driven; successful relationships are not his first priority. Sometimes successful coaching can occur without this; many Premiership cups are testament to this.

Successful mentors have sound relationships, built on trust, honesty and listening with open communication. This can be subtle and sometimes mentors are not even aware that they are mentoring. Take, for example, the older sibling who teaches the younger brother or sister the dangers of a busy road. This sibling would be driven by their innate desire to protect the younger one because of their love and care, not a desire to be a good mentor—yet their action demonstrates what mentoring is.

Great mentors affirm the potential of their athletes. They also share their own adversities and frustrations—or how they overcame their obstacles, if it's relevant to the personal growth of the athlete. This must not be confused with telling someone how things must be done or the 'back in my day, this is how we did it' approach. If mentoring is based on respect, then comments such as this infer that 'we did it better and you don't know much', which can negate mutual respect and the whole idea of developing the person as well as the athlete. Why would someone attempt to improve or take risks if they were always thought to be inferior to previous methods and styles?

Past ideas and experiences are to be respected—they often show how things developed—but they must be seen as belonging to another time. Many methods used in the past were deemed progressive but, like everything in our technological world, they are soon superseded and new methods take over.

Many years ago, in the marathon at the Olympic games, fluid intake was limited throughout the race. If it was consumed, some viewed it as a form of cheating. Now that view is unheard of and athletes are encouraged to drink before and throughout the event to prevent dehydration and a drop-off in performance.

In relation to injuries, it was once thought that when a player had an acute injury, heat should be applied to the area, using a heat lamp or liniment. The practitioners of that time were correct in addressing the injury, but the remedy used was incorrect. Today the specific area is still addressed, but ice is directly applied with compression to reduce internal bleeding. Research and risk-taking made room for the new to be built upon the old.

The most important aspect of being a mentor is developing trust. Why would Darren Crocker follow David's instructions and get into an ice bath, a method he had never heard of before, if he did not have trust in his coach? And why would players go into the caves of Mole Creek in Tasmania, crawling through tight crevices and experiencing claustrophobia, if they did not have trust in Mick as their coach? It's because, over time, they have developed faith and respect for the person who is guiding them. Experience has shown that the one guiding them has their best interests at heart and would not put them under duress if they did not have a good reason. Simply, their merit has been proven by actions.

Chris Dawes—Watching role models

Watching Luke Ball training and being so humble and professional was very impressive. But what was more noticeable was that he wasn't trying to prove anything to anyone—he was doing it for himself. He's a great example of a good role model.

Above: White Christmas, 2008.
From left: Dylan, Emily, Maria, Bronte,
Nicholas and David Buttifant

Right: Bronte Buttifant and Mick
Malthouse, Club Christmas Function,
2004

The Malthouse family at daughter Danielle's wedding to Simon,
December 2008. From left: Cain, Nanette, Mick, Danielle, Simon, Christi,
Dean (holding 10-day-old Zac), Troy and Talia

Ben Cousins and
Mick Malthouse, 1999.
Image courtesy of
George Salpigtidis/©
Newspix/News Ltd.

Wayne Carey, Kangaroos, and Glen Jakovich, Eagles, chasing the ball at the
Sydney Cricket Ground, 14 June 1999. Image courtesy Getty Images.

Mick Malthouse, David Buttifant and players ascending Mt Humphreys, 2005

Players and staff resting on the saddle of Mt Humphreys before ascending to the peak, 2006

Sedona, Arizona, 2006. From left: Guy McKenna, David Buttifant and Brad Scott

First year's camp, Mole Creek, Tasmania before commencing the caving expedition, 2007. From left: David Buttifant, Brad Dick, Brent Macaffer, Chris Dawes, Tyson Goldsack, Martin Clarke, Sharrod Wellingham, Ben Reid, Nathan Brown, Simon Lloyd and Mick Malthouse

Caving at Mole Creek, 'the squeeze test' with the first year's camp, 2007

First year's camp, Dove Lake, Tasmania, 2007. Recovery swim after hiking up to Cradle Mountain. From left: Mick Malthouse, Nathan Brown, Brent Macaffer, Chris Dawes, Tyson Goldsack, Brad Dick, Sharrod Wellingham, Martin Clarke, Ben Reid, David Buttifant and Simon Lloyd

Mick Malthouse viewing Tugela Falls, Drakensberg in KwaZulu-Natal Province, South Africa, 2007. It is the second highest waterfall in the world.

David Buttifant and kids, Soweto, South Africa, January 2008

David Buttifant and young baby at an orphanage outside Soweto, South Africa, January 2008

David Buttifant and Eddie McGuire at the resting point on the descent of Mt Humphreys, 2008

Resting near the peak of Mt Humphreys in minus 35 degrees, 2009. From left: Cameron Wood, Sharrod Wellingham and Chris Dawes

Players descending Mt Humphreys in minus 35 degrees, 2009

Mick Malthouse and David Buttifant on the Sedona, Arizona Mountain Bike Trail, 2010

Grand Canyon hike, players and staff, 2010

Players and staff commencing the ascent of Mt Humphreys, 2010. From left: Paul Licuria, Steele Sidebottom, David Buttifant, Tom Hunter, Alan Toovey and Justin Crow

Mick Malthouse,
David Buttifant and
Paul Licuria watch
the training at the
Skydome, Northern
Arizona University,
Flagstaff, 2010

Mick Malthouse explaining a training drill to the playing group, at the
Skydome, Northern Arizona University, Flagstaff, 2010

Mick with the team after the drawn Grand Final, 2010

Leon Davis and
Mick Malthouse,
2010. Image
courtesy of
Michael Dodge/©
Newspix/News
Ltd.

Grand Final Celebration, 2010. From left: David Buttifant, Harry O'Brien and Paul Licuria. Image courtesy of Paul Rovere/Fairfax Syndication.

Dane Swan donating a car to the N.I.C.K. Foundation, 2010. David and Emily Buttifant on either side. Image courtesy of Cameron L'Estrange/ Fotogroup.

Westpac Centre promoting the N.I.C.K. Foundation, 2011.
From left: Sharrod Wellingham, Dane Swan, Alan Didak, David Buttifant,
Harry O'Brien and Mick Malthouse

David Buttifant and Mick Malthouse discussing training loads at Gosch's
Paddock, 2011

Harry O'Brien winning the 2 km time trial, January 2011. Nathan Buckley and David Buttifant in background

Mick Malthouse and David Buttifant, first year's camp, Mt Kosciuszko, 2011

A young player arriving at a club follows directions without question because he sees the older players following instructions without hesitation. It's often through demonstration that trust and a genuine understanding for a person is established and this can galvanise into a fruitful relationship. But trust is not easy to acquire, and once it is lost, it may never be gained again.

David—Blue Mountains 2001

A small party of 16 players and staff went on a leadership camp to the Blue Mountains in New South Wales in early 2001. This involved hiking, canyoning and abseiling, all with some degree of difficulty and technicality. As with all camps, the group was given a comprehensive brief on the safety measures, dangers and emergency procedures beforehand. Decked out with wetsuit-like clothing, abseiling harnesses and other necessary equipment, the party set out on the six-hour expedition.

The guides were ex-SAS personnel and when they knew they were taking elite athletes on a trek, they made sure that it was challenging. The hike took us through some beautiful but treacherous terrain and into underground water tunnels where our heads were barely above the water level. We were required to independently abseil down sheer waterfalls of approximately 30 metres. We were expected to be responsible for attaching each other's equipment and ensuring that the ropes were secure enough to take the weight of our partners. There was naturally some trepidation, as we had to have complete trust in one another. However, as we progressed we became better at the skills and at using the equipment and we developed confidence in one another. The trust within the group escalated as we achieved each challenge and I was pleased to observe the dialogue and support each person demonstrated.

Sometimes, though, when one becomes confident with a skill or an activity, complacency sets in. This may be fine in some circumstances, but when the situation involves potential danger, there's no room for complacency. As we progressed through the final stages of the expedition we were walking along a path no wider than half a metre. To the left of this path was a rock wall and to the right a sheer drop. The group was coping well with this until we came to a ravine—a break in the path—that we had to cross, which was a metre wide and had a drop of several metres.

Making this landing may not sound too difficult considering what we had already accomplished. However, what exacerbated our fears was the fact that we were no longer roped up. As we approached the ravine we were in single file, led by Anthony Rocca. The path wasn't wide enough for more than one at a time. Rocca asked the guide if we could rope up. The guide declined and told us we would be fine. He further suggested that it could be easy once the first person got across, as they could guide the others by grabbing their hands. I could see anxiety and apprehension on the players' faces because, like me, they could see the catastrophic consequences of not making the landing. Rocca flatly refused and I knew there was no choice; it was going to have to be me!

I was no less nervous than the others. If I jumped and accidently bumped the rock wall on the left, I could have lost my balance and fallen down to the right, which was not a comforting thought. I began to question the judgement of our guides, but it was my turn to place my trust in them. This camp was the first camp I'd attended at Collingwood and I knew I had to gain the trust of the playing group. If the guides said it could be completed without ropes, then complete it unaided I would. So I reluctantly volunteered to go first.

I focussed on the landing, as well as a position on the wall where I could stabilise myself. With many pairs of eyes on me, I jumped. I realised that my trust in the guides had been justified. The jump was not as threatening as I had first thought. The challenge wasn't so difficult; it was simply the drop ahead combined with that on the side that had played with my mind.

After I landed safely, I turned to the players and reassured them that it was fine. I told them that I would grab them as they reached the other side to secure their landing. Rocca led the rest of the group and they successfully achieved the task.

A good listener is someone who actually hears beyond the words that are being spoken; good listeners gain the trust of others. At Collingwood the sports-science team use a monitoring system to see where athletes are at in their day-to-day wellbeing. For example, they may notice that a player's sleep patterns are abnormal. Their initial explanation for this could be 'overloading'. A discussion with key personnel would follow, where life in general is discussed.

In this casual chat, several things may be subtly revealed. For example, an inquiry into how their girlfriend is going may lead to a nonchalant reply, such as, 'Yeah, not bad.' This could be clue enough to lead the discussion into inquiring if everything is okay at home. By this stage, the player might openly confide that they are having a few problems and that late-night arguments are causing sleep disturbances.

But being a good listener goes one step further. A player who shares something about himself has usually selected this person because they consider them to be a confidant. Therefore, they are looking for a non-judgemental ear. They need to say what they have to say without feeling like they are being judged. They may need some advice or direction and this is why they are sharing their thoughts, but they're not in a position or frame of mind to be chastised or lectured. Generally they already know that they have made an error or are in need of assistance. It doesn't help to hear 'I told you so!' after they have shared some personal information. The art of mentoring is to learn to listen without judging, yet still guide the mentee in the right direction. A skilled mentor will have learnt the art of helping their mentee find the answer for themselves.

Once a good relationship has been established, the mentor can openly provide constructive feedback and more specific discussions of strengths and weaknesses. For some it's hard to accept home truths and they might resist progress. But once the athlete accepts that their mentor is there to help them develop as an athlete and, more importantly, as a person, growth is inevitable.

The key is honesty. Although an athlete may not want to hear that they have to develop a stronger work ethic, for example, if they have a solid relationship with their mentor they will accept this feedback. They may respond negatively at first because they don't want to hear it, but they will eventually accept it because the relationship is such a trusted one—they know the comment was given for their benefit and that the mentor only hopes to guide them positively.

At those times in our lives when we search for answers and struggle to resolve problems, we often turn to someone with experience and wisdom simply for reassurance and hope. We don't always get the answer we are looking for, but often positive encouragement provides all the tonic we need.

Alan Didak—Mentors

I've met a few people who were older than me and taught me a lot on the value of family and life. I'm so grateful to have those people in my life.

We often see successful young sportspeople who have been guided by solid, caring mentors graduate into positions of leadership themselves. This may be in sport as coaches or as managing directors in business. This is no coincidence.

Mick—Acorn to oak

I first watched Glen Jakovich when he was a 16-year-old playing at centre half-forward for the Western Australia Football League club South Fremantle. He played state football all through his teenage years and when we (at West Coast) had the chance to take him in the 1990 draft we took it.

This kid was all over the shop, though. His father died when he was 15, leaving an indelible mark. His older brother Allen was a superstar in the West Australian and Northern Territory leagues as a full-forward, giving the younger brother the impression that he had high expectations to live up to. He was confident in himself and his own abilities, but lacked accountability.

What I had vowed to do at West Coast was create a solid defence for the game plan to be based around. The question with Glen then was: would he add to or detract from this?

I made him wait. I watched him and watched him. I played others, like Ashley McIntosh, in front of him. I made it clear there would be no easy entrance into the AFL, especially not straight into the forward line, where he was used to playing and could use his natural abilities but might easily forget the team mantra of defence. I wanted to see how he would react. I am pleased to say that he reacted in a manner well beyond his years.

On 9 June 1991 he was ready. It was Round 12, we were playing the Brisbane Bears at Carrara Stadium and I played Glen at centre half-back. He filled the position so well he was never dropped again under my coaching. The wait had paid off.

When I first played him on Wayne Carey—the North Melbourne centre half-forward who is remembered as one of the greats of the game—I told Glen that as he was roughly the same age as Carey he would probably play on him for the rest of his career. This made it important that he establish dominance at the very beginning. He had to challenge Carey away from his natural game, which was leading—forward, backward, sideways—and take him on with his own strengths. Weighing in at 100 kilograms, it was no wonder Glen couldn't be beaten at ground-level contests. So this is where he asserted himself and won.

The Jakovich–Carey duels would become among the most highly anticipated clashes of each football season and, more often than not, Glen would have the upper hand.

I can remember, however, twice when he didn't win and why he didn't. Before a game in 1994 I noticed that Glen was very agitated. When I asked him why he said, 'This is such an important game, I know if I don't beat Carey we won't win the game.' That worried me. Wayne Carey (five goals) played his best-ever game against Glen to beat him, but we still won the match convincingly.

Afterwards I said, 'Let this be a lesson to you Glen.' I told him that by focussing on himself too much rather than the team he let himself and the team down, which led to an ordinary performance. He needed to play his part without worrying about being everything to everyone. He could help the team and the team could help him. Lesson learnt.

On another occasion Carey was left out of the North Melbourne team due to injury and his replacement was Mark (Fridge) Roberts. Glen seemed to be thinking: 'I've beaten Carey, Brownless, Schwarz. Who the hell is Mark Roberts?' Underrating anyone is a mistake. Mark Roberts played a best-on-ground performance that day, with 24 disposals and 3 goals.

It was another great life lesson for this young player who would go on to be one of the greats of the game himself. Glen won numerous club champion awards, was twice named as All Australian and was inducted into the AFL Hall of Fame in 1998.

In the time I've known him Glen has gone from being a kid to a husband, to a father and now a businessman.

Glen and his brother Allen were chalk and cheese in their dedication to establishing themselves as AFL footballers. Allen had success in the AFL, but what differentiates a good player from a great player is how they respond in the heat of the battle, especially when the chips are down.

Glen learnt on a week-to-week basis about himself and about life. When he began, he had an extraordinary ambition to succeed. When ill-directed, ambition can be dangerous. Ambition can absorb you and overtake your thinking. You become selfish instead of selfless.

Glen learnt instead about teamwork and to be team-oriented. In 1994, we were to play Melbourne in a preliminary final. They had just come off a huge win over Footscray, in which Garry Lyon and David Schwarz had dominated. I spoke to Glen before our game about his role in the final. His sole focus was to destroy Schwarz's confidence early and keep him away from the ball as much as possible. This would mean being totally defensive. On his debut, Glen had gone from centre half-forward to playing at centre half-back because that was the best option for the team. In this instance, too, he needed to be defensive first and attacking second because this would mean the best result for the team. He understood his role and played it with maturity. He destroyed Schwarz, keeping him goalless, and then attacked. We won and made it through to the grand final, 16.21 (117) to 8.4 (52).

Almost a year after Glen came to West Coast, his mother, Margaret, called to thank me for being a father-figure to Glen. It was a great pleasure to be involved in the development of that young man. We remain friends today and he has worked alongside me in the coaches' box for the Australian International Rules team.

Glen Jakovich—Mick's influence on me

When my father passed away in my teenage years I had no figurehead. I was playing at South Fremantle and my football was going quite well. My goal was to get drafted. Mick kept me firmly planted on the ground and I knew where I stood being coached by him.

I had had a lot of recognition as a junior and Mick gave me a wonderful opportunity, but he was my harshest critic. He eradicated my bad habits from my junior days and developed me into a better footballer and a better person. My life changed positively due to Mick's influence on me.

My formative years were shaped by Mick and I was a sponge to learn more about the game. He straightened me out as a person and I'm grateful for that. He gave me some big challenges—such as putting me on Wayne Carey. It was hard mentoring, but if I didn't have that challenge then it wouldn't have stretched me. It was character-building.

Just as Odysseus requested Mentor to impart his knowledge and wisdom onto his son, mentors in sport, as well as in life, are successful when they nurture with the view to

empowering people to become well-rounded individuals—
individuals who, in turn, develop mentoring skills and go on
to help others.

CHAPTER 7

WHAT MAKES THEM TICK

As AFL players are selected by particular clubs through the national draft, it goes without saying that new personal relationships are suddenly thrust upon them. To start with, there are relationships with the recruiting and management teams at the new club. If you're a forward-line player, you would not only work under the head coach but also the forward-line coach and the conditioning staff would guide your fitness. If you get injured, you work with the medical and rehabilitation team. Of course, if a team from another state selects you, *all* your relationships change, including those away from the club. It also goes without saying that good relationships are the cornerstone of any sporting team.

Intuition

As relationships develop, intuition guides a greater understanding of each other, although this is often not noticed or recognised at the time. Awareness of idiosyncrasies, body language, tone of voice, energy levels and general engagement become clearer; our decisions about people are often made emotionally from these feeds—following gut feelings—and can lack any rational process.

Sometimes these decisions are accurate, but sometimes we are caught off-guard and discover we've got it wrong. For example, junior players may have negative experiences with their coaches. These experiences remain very clear in their minds as they develop. Later, they may have other coaches who, from the beginning, have similar outward characteristics; a similar voice or expression may bring back their earlier negative reactions. An immediate dislike can occur by association and it may take the young player some time to discover that the new coach is quite different.

Generally, though, our initial opinion is right and our gut feeling doesn't let us down. Why is it that we mostly get it right? Why is it that sometimes we feel that we shouldn't walk down a particular street or trust a person who has knocked on our door? It's a difficult question to answer, but sometimes we just know! Similarly, there's often no rhyme or reason to the quality of the relationships that develop between players and coaches. Sometimes the relationship is not working, but at other times—just like with Goldilocks— 'It's juuust right!'

David—Initial meeting with Nick Maxwell

In 2002 our previous recruiting manager, Noel Judkin, introduced a young fresh-faced boy from Ocean Grove to me at Victoria Park. The old adage 'first impressions are lasting impressions' rang true. His natural enthusiasm, inquisitiveness, politeness and sense of inner confidence left an indelible mark on me. Without performing any testing or even viewing his game edits it was clear that this kid had something. I couldn't pinpoint anything specific; it might have been his desire to play AFL coupled with his 'knowledge' that he would succeed, I wasn't sure. Of course, at the time I didn't even entertain the thought that he would one day become a Premiership captain or be selected as an All Australian. I took in what I saw and for no apparent reason felt high achievement was inevitable for Nick. I knew that this kid was going places and time would tell that I was right!

This type of assessment of people may seem to have little place in a world where scientific systems determine so much about the decisions that are made about players. From the moment a player is being looked at for recruitment, a mass of data is collected—from physiological and psychological profiling to performance statistics to GPS assessment of total game distance run and average game running velocity. Down the track, this data is not just for the recruitment and selection of players, it's relayed regularly to coaches on game day, influencing their decisions as the game proceeds.

Often there are times, though, when quick assessments and snap decisions need to be made. In these cases, it's likely that we rely on our intuition for rapid judgement and action. In times when decisions need to be made quickly, there's no time to waste—such as game day, where the coach has to make snap decisions and moves to win the game. There's little time to deliberate and action needs to be delivered promptly. During high-pressure games, all senses are on high alert and a lot of information is being digested, so it's important to remain clear-headed for effective decision-making.

Intuition or gut feel is drawn upon regularly throughout sport. The greater the experience the coach has, the broader the repertoire of scenarios he can draw upon to assist with this decision-making. And the more coaches within a team who have this experience, the better. It is even more effective when these coaches have worked together for some time, because their experience goes beyond just being an individual one, but a collective one.

Mick—Gut feelings on moves in a game

In the 1992 grand final between West Coast and Geelong, the Cats got off to a flyer against us. Just before half-time I made a decision to move Brett Heady onto Paul Couch. It was a risky move as Brett had never played a tagging role and was, in fact, used to playing only in the forward line. He was also recovering from a hamstring injury, so the extra running would test him.

But we needed to do something. Couch was dominating in the midfield, which was hurting us badly. His original opponent, Craig Turley, was struggling to curb his ascendancy and ball-getting ability.

The decision to run Brett with him instead was, in many respects, a gut feel. Most of the Cats' midfield players relied heavily on their instinct to win the ball, with little attention paid to their direct opponent. They were very offensively minded. My instructions for Brett were simple. Couch would take him to the ball and then he was to use his own strength and knowledge to win the 50/50 contests. Brett had an attacking instinct that would enable him to be an offensive weapon as well as a close-down player.

The effect was immediate. Couch no longer dominated and it freed up our prime midfielders, Peter Matera (who was best on ground by the end of the match), Dean Kemp and Tony Evans and wingmen Chris Mainwaring and Chris Waterman. All of these players were able to maximise Brett's defensive aspects and started to take charge of the contested and uncontested possessions.

We won the Premiership. It wasn't that single move that did it, but it certainly helped.

In 2010, in the first grand final between Collingwood and St Kilda, Lenny Hayes was inspirational for the Saints. He was the standout player of the game. Luke Ball (a former St Kilda teammate of Hayes) played on him.

In the replay, there was concern within the club that Hayes would again take control, though we stuck to our guns and kept the match-up the same.

Why didn't we try someone new on Hayes? Because Luke had demonstrated a great willingness to redeem himself. He had been vulnerable the previous week, feeling a little overawed at playing in a grand final against his former teammates. His strength of character wouldn't let it happen again and we trusted that.

As it turned out, Luke was brilliant. He managed to quell the influence of Hayes while working tirelessly to gather effective possessions himself.

He wasn't the only one working smart and hard.

Brendon Goddard was another stand-out for the Saints the Saturday before and he was again proving difficult to keep down. We had designated two players (Nick Maxwell and Alan Toovey) to work in tandem wherever Goddard played, midfield or forward. Neither player really proved successful, although we led well at half time, 6.5–1.8.

As the Collingwood players emerged from our player–coach discussion at half time, I made a spur-of-the-moment decision. Call it another gut feeling, if you like.

I decided to put Dane Swan (who was going okay, but not at his usual dominant best) onto their prime mover, Goddard.

This could have backfired if Dane's own game became compromised by the tagging role, but I had faith in him and his abilities. Plus I also had history to rely on. In previous drawn grand finals the top players from each club rarely performed at the same level in the replay. There are a number of reasons for this, though I would say that the effort required to attain such a great height drains the player mentally and physically.

We not only needed history on our side, but good strategies in place too. The Dane Swan move had not been discussed during the week. But the hunch paid off.

Dane was able to work well both offensively and defensively against Goddard. He still had the flair to attack when needed, while Goddard's dominance was reduced. It may have been a hasty move, but it was a decisive one.

Again we won the Premiership and the Luke Ball–Lenny Hayes and Dane Swan—Brendon Goddard match-ups were key to the victory.

In a football match, many moves are made every quarter. Some of them are planned, some are made on instinct and others are on a whim. Most decisions are made in a split-second. Footy moves at a very fast pace and waits for no one to be settled.

By keeping the bigger picture in mind when making decisions along the way, you can be more decisive. If it doesn't work, you may need to change back quickly to reduce any damage done. However, if the scoreboard isn't ticking over, wait to see if the move matures. Sometimes persistence has its own reward.

Experience, knowledge, intuition and an insight into recent history will help you to make the right moves. Trust yourself and back yourself, but never be afraid to ask for another opinion and support.

Knowing your athlete

Dealing with athletes on a daily basis allows you to observe their idiosyncrasies over time. The subtle physical cues that athletes display in various circumstances can assist with formulating a subjective behavioural profile. Body language, in particular, should be noted.

David—Dane Swan and the drawn grand final

Dane Swan, commonly known as Swanny, is the most relaxed player I have ever worked with. He rarely gets anxious or fazed about any game, even a blockbuster. Before high-pressure games his demeanour is nonchalant—he's 'cool as a cucumber'. But while his mood levels are even-keeled in the change rooms, he maintains an inner focus beneath his walk, his larrikin smile, his quick wit and trademark coolness.

Two hours before the drawn grand final I noticed a slight change in Swanny's disposition and was concerned. Anxiety prior to a grand final is hardly surprising, but from my experience with Swanny, it was slightly off-centre.

After observing him closely for some time it dawned on me that Swanny had had a huge week—a week bigger than that of many other players. He had been the favourite for the Brownlow Medal but had missed out on the award. With all the media hype and commitments that came with that, his attention had been distracted from his usual preparation. I felt it must have had some effect on him.

I approached him and had a brief chat to sense how he was going. He appeared to be parading his usual antics, but it was not the same Swanny. I could see that the week had drained him and I knew he would not be firing on all cylinders.

Swanny was serviceable throughout the game, but he was not his normal dominating self. The team was given another chance the following week and it was then that I saw him transform back to the Swanny of old. The distractions were firmly in the past and a clear path was set. In the second grand final he definitely fired on all cylinders.

This slight behavioural change in Swanny on the eve of the drawn grand final was noted, but unfortunately it was too late to intervene and try to help. The key would have been to pick it up earlier in the week and attempt to minimise his distractions.

Dane Swan—Drawn grand final week

The week was full-on. Every day I had to wear a suit—it just wasn't normal, it wasn't my scene. Being the perceived favourite for the Brownlow

and all the external pressure made it so unnecessary. I felt a bit embarrassed not winning as
everyone expected me to win. I was relieved it was
all over and I just wanted to focus on the game. At
the end of the game I was just overwhelmed—I
thought, 'Wow! Who would have picked that?' I
felt like laughing; it was such a weird feeling. But
reflecting back, I was still rapt to be involved.

Motivation

Many people who work with athletes spend a lot of time
trying to work out what makes them tick. What induces
them to strive for greater heights? Metaphorically speaking,
is it the carrot dangling ahead of them or the bamboo stick
threatening from behind? So many AFL footballers display
similar qualities, but it's the unique characteristics of each
individual and how each man becomes motivated that separate them from one another.

Nathan Buckley—What motivates you?

The thing that motivates me is bringing a group
of individuals together to succeed. It's about being
a good example and helping the group. When I
retired I realised it was all about the group; I had
just wanted to be a part of the group and have
a positive influence on them. Whether you're a
player or a coach there's a great fulfilment in being
a part of the team.

It is generally accepted that elite sportspeople are highly
motivated individuals. But what makes the 'high flyer' fly
even higher? Why do some athletes seek responsibility and

have a burning desire to achieve, while others are passive and avoid responsibility? This intangible drive is difficult to define. Sometimes inspiration can come from a special place—from the daring and sacrifice of others.

Mick—The significance of the ANZAC Day game

The Anzac Day clash between Collingwood and Essendon is one of my favourite games of each season.

The big crowds, the media and supporter-driven build-up and the memory of past encounters make for a blockbuster experience. Being involved in the event as a coach makes it all the more exciting and memorable; I'm deeply privileged to have been involved in these MCG games since the year 2000.

However, as a historian and a proud Australian, I've cherished being a part of Anzac Day football because of the real significance of Anzac Day. Many soldiers serving in Gallipoli and every other war since (including the current battles in Afghanistan and Iraq) have lost their lives or been severely injured. Their families and loved ones have been left to grieve. This is true sacrifice. For the teams participating in the Anzac Day game, it's a chance to honour those courageous and selfless members of our armed forces. Our sacrifice is little, but our respect is great.

I believe Anzac Day to be the most important and proudest day on the Australian footy calendar. This is reflected by the enormity of the Anzac Day match in the AFL season. The game itself is dwarfed by the occasion. We are fortunate to play a game of AFL football on this day—25 April—and it's important we realise why we honour the significance of this date with such a match. An AFL grand final at the MCG can hold nearly 100,000 supporters. The Anzac Day game is the only other football contest that has a chance of reaching this attendance number. The MCC committee is as proud to hold the game as we are to play in it.

I remember an Anzac Day game long weekend when I was coach of the West Coast Eagles; we were playing a match at Waverley Park. I wanted my players to recognise that this was a tradition like no other. The actual Anzac Day clash is not necessarily played between the best teams of the competition each year and yet, for a home-and-away game, it has a finals-like atmosphere.

I therefore wanted my team to feel some of that sense of occasion and for the players involved to know the true significance of the contest. So I took several globes out of the fixtures on the ceiling of our change rooms to dim the light in the room. We watched a video depicting the atrocities faced by the brave Anzacs on the coastline of Turkey in World War I and we had a discussion about fighting spirit and sacrifice.

I'm not sure what the players thought about this, but I hope they were positively affected by the message I was trying to convey about the importance of the match we were preparing to play in.

When I finally came to be involved in Anzac Day games (played on the actual date) with Collingwood, I made it my mission to also teach the Magpie players about the Anzac story. I felt it was my obligation to enlighten another generation of young men about the battles faced by our Australian and New Zealand Army Corps troops in World War I.

Each year I told the team, 'We must never forget the sacrifices of our Anzac heroes, nor of any other Australian, man or woman, who has served in our armed forces.'

The Collingwood players were made aware of who they were representing on the day and why.

We would attend our own private dawn service during the week leading up to the game. (More than once we insisted that the young players not participating in the game attend the memorial dawn service on Anzac Day.) We would stand at the Shrine of Remembrance listening to the 'Last Post' being played on the bugle and think about the courage of those soldiers under fierce attack on the coast of Gallipoli. We would ponder the thousands of causalities and the loved ones left grieving. We were inspired by the Anzac Legend—the 'never give up' attitude of that brave army. By the morning of the match we were ready to pay true respect to the men and women who have fought for our country since the landing at Gallipoli.

The Anzac Day match, therefore, is a timely reminder of our country's fighting past (and present). When a player excels on the battlefield of the Melbourne Cricket Ground on this day, it is because he is filled with the spirit of the Anzacs. This is a lesson that can never be forgotten.

Of all the awards on offer in our game—the Brownlow, Norm Smith and Coleman medals—it's the Anzac Day Medal that perhaps has the most profound effect on the recipient. As well as being judged the best on ground, it is his exemplification of the Anzac spirit—skill, courage, self-sacrifice, teamwork and fair play—that the award stands for. From the last decade, the medal-winner that most resonates with me is Mark McGough in 2002. It was only his second game of AFL and he was just 17 years old—the same age as so many of the soldiers who enlisted and were deployed to Gallipoli. He is no doubt remembered more for this than for any other match of his 46-game career.

We realise that football is not life and death. We know it's only a sporting contest. We understand that each game that is played on Anzac Day will quickly be forgotten. We are aware that the Anzac Day Medallist will be regularly reminded about how he played on that particular day, not necessarily why he played. As the match fades, though, the Anzac Day tradition must never diminish.

Standing out in the middle of the Melbourne Cricket Ground on Anzac Day, two teams ready to face off, the unique sound of the 'Last Post' being played on the bugle will remind them of why they are there. The game that follows will reflect how they honour our soldiers. The crowd will see the best the players have to offer as the Anzac spirit inspires them. It will leave a powerful imprint on our memory, one that for me will last forever.

'We will remember them.'

'Ode of Remembrance (For The Fallen)',
Laurence Binyon, 1914.

Many athletes with motivation and a great desire to achieve are driven by the lure of the carrots dangled in front of them: success, wealth and accomplishment. Some, on the other hand, are driven by the stick behind them, which can present itself as fear of failure, the fear of not living up to other people's expectations or even their own standards. The difference between the carrot and the stick motivations can be found in the goals that people set for themselves.

What motivates you?
Ben Reid

The fear of failure motivates me, particularly for everyone who has helped me and been involved with me.

Chris Dawes

I want to be the best and to show and prove to myself that I can be the best. It is truly remarkable that five out of the seven of us who started in 2007 have done what we've done! I'm not too sure what motivates them, but I've always dreamed that I'd play in an AFL Premiership. I did have doubts towards the end of 2010 season. I worried I was going to be dropped, but that motivated me to push on and not miss out. I wanted so much to be a part of it.

Luke Ball

The risk of losing the respect of my teammates and helping them to succeed motivates me.

Scott Pendlebury

I like to set high goals and I like to achieve them.

Many athletes at Collingwood aiming for the carrot have been motivated by the prospect of success and they tend to choose challenging yet reachable goals. This means that success is possible, but not so easy as to be trivial. The ones who are motivated by fear of failure, on the other hand, either choose extremely easy goals so that they won't fail or fall so far or set extremely difficult goals, so that when they fail they can blame their goal as being unreasonable and unreachable. Goal-setting needs to be realistic and progressive.

David—Harry O'Brien's actions

In 2005, Collingwood's national recruiting manager, Derek Hine, approached me about a potential rookie-list player. This was not uncommon; we regularly discussed potential players. But what was different in this situation was that the young player in question, Harry O'Brien from Perth, had not been successful in the recent national draft. As a result, he had rung the club and spoken to Derek with a proposal. He had asked Derek that if he paid his own fare and found his own accommodation in Melbourne, could he train with the squad. After discussion with Derek, we decided that this would not compromise our training or current playing group and agreed that he could come over and train for one week. The young player showed some initiative and, for all we knew, it could end up being a benefit to us.

Harry moved over and joined the squad in training. We were impressed with his dedication, his athleticism and skills, as well as his passion to play AFL. After two weeks of trialling Harry we decided to put him on our rookie list. Harry showed much promise and later that preseason he was elevated to the senior list. He had achieved his first goal.

One of the next goals Harry set was to play a senior game—an accomplishment he worked hard to achieve. Further to this, he aimed to finish in the top five in the best and fairest, as well as aiming to win the two-kilometre time trial and the speed endurance test. Harry is now on the leadership team and has the title of All Australian under his list of achievements, as well as an AFL Premiership. Harry went on to achieve his goals with a progressive approach.

Harry O'Brien—On planning

I work on three principles. Firstly, passion and belief that everything is possible. Secondly, you need to have a purpose that gives you the fuel to achieve your goal. Finally, you need to put it into action. You have to walk the walk.

Harry was realistic in what he aimed for. His first aim was to make the list. It was not to be a Premiership player (although that would have been in his bigger picture). Harry held on to his larger goals while achieving his smaller ones. The goal-setting that is applied at Collingwood aims to be dynamic and empower the athlete. It is not purely driven by goal-setting outcomes but, more importantly, by the *process of goal-setting*. The goal-planning procedures within the football department are not just for documenting goals; they are about interpersonal skills, timing, creative thinking and overcoming logistical limitations. None of this goal-setting is effective, however, if the coach doesn't know the athlete and the athlete doesn't know himself.

Ambition

Why is it that some people have greater drive than others? Many talented footballers come through Collingwood's program and not make it. Talent is essential and tends to be genetically inherited—in other words, they've chosen their parents wisely. But talent is not everything! Those athletes who have blended their talent with their need to succeed have been able to achieve a lot more, as Harry has.

Ambition is a term flippantly used among athletes to describe their desire for success. But so often the athlete has a misconception of what ambition actually is. Commonly it's thought to encompass characteristics such as desire, dreams, purpose and aspiration—and so it does, to some degree. But these definitions are inadequate.

Genuine ambition is inbuilt and associated with an increase in adrenaline. As with the 'fight or flight' response, there's a choice to be made: to flee or to stay and fight. Both will cause an automatic physiological response, but only the latter will centre its sole attention on succeeding. A mother who shows amazing courage and strength to lift an extreme weight in dangerous, life-threatening circumstances—such as when the safety of her child is at stake—draws from a mysterious pool. Similarly, from somewhere within the elite athlete's psyche comes an inborn surge of ambition in the shape of adrenaline as strong as a hunger that must be fed or a thirst that must be quenched. It's not until the food or drink is ingested that the surge abates. For the ambitious athlete it only recedes when the goals they have set are achieved. Ambition can regress when an athlete is confronted with setbacks or challenges, but those who possess genuine ambition will not allow setbacks or challenges to derail their dream.

There can be danger accompanying ambition, as truly ambitious people sometimes bend the rules to achieve their goal. We only need to look at the Tour de France and see how often cyclists have tested positive to performance enhancing drugs. Similarly, several track-and-field athletes (such as Canadian Ben Johnson and American Marion Jones) have been found guilty of using banned substances. These athletes had genuine ambition but were so ambitious to win that they compromised themselves and those they represented.

In such cases, unfettered ambition came at a cost because athletes are more than just individuals; they are always a part of something greater. At some point the dream of becoming an Olympic champion existed in these athletes and their training and methods were ethical. But blind ambition clouded their approach and they took a wrong turn; the individuals became so overrun by their ambition that they needed to succeed at all costs.

How does an athlete avoid the trap of becoming so focussed on winning that they begin to cheat? Have such people forgotten why they are playing sport in the first place? Why does any young child play a sport? More often than not it is because they love it. Yes, they relish the competitiveness, but they can remain true to themselves by staying within the rules. Surely you no longer love your sport when you degrade it by winning illegitimately. Athletes must remember that they are a part of a bigger picture: their team, club and family. The common element young athletes have is their love of their sport and their teammates. In other words, they're a part of a bigger picture and recognise their value as a spoke in the wheel—just like the mother who finds that incredible strength when needed to save her child. A greater force is driving her—her ambition is part of a bigger picture: her love of her family.

Most respected athletes recognise their role in the bigger picture. They remain true to themselves and trust the methods that work for them, even in times of adversity. They do not deviate from this process.

David—Simon Prestigiacomo and the 2010 grand final

Every team is made up of a vast range of players and characters with various ability levels. Simon Prestigiacomo has owned Collingwood Football Club's position of full-back for the last 14 years. Every week he executed his role as a defender by negating the opposition's most potent offensive players. He had only scored three goals in his AFL career and averaged fewer than ten possessions a game, which hardly looks like a glamorous statistic. But these statistics in no way reflect the importance of Simon's role. Among his fellow players he was extremely valued as an important spoke in the wheel—he was once voted the most valued player in the team by his teammates.

Presti, as he is known, is one of the quietest men you will meet in a sporting team. Following our last training session on the eve of the first 2010 grand final, Presti asked if he could speak with Mick after training. As this was very unusual for Presti, we were alarmed and concerned. Mick and I found Presti with the physiotherapist Gary Nicholls in his office. As we entered the room we noticed that Gary was assessing Presti's groin and immediately read the look on his face. We knew things weren't good. While this was happening, the rest of the players were preparing for the Grand Final Parade.

It's a long-standing tradition in Melbourne that on the eve of the AFL grand final, the players and coaches of both teams parade through the city streets. By lunchtime on the last Friday in September, the streets are blocked off to make way for the procession. The streets are lined with well over 100,000 cheering supporters, rain, hail or shine, all hoping to get a glimpse of their heroes. Any Collingwood supporter would have looked at Presti with his two children by his side and imagined him taking on the opposition's hero and captain, Nick Reiwoldt, the next day, totally unaware of what had transpired less than an hour before.

As Mick and I stood in Gary's office, I asked what was going on. Gary explained that two days earlier, Presti had had an incident at the main training session. He had felt sore but hoped it would settle down by Friday. He had now come to see Gary because it had not settled; he was also aware of a lack of power in his adductor muscle.

All of us were very concerned for him and encouraged him not to panic or to make a decision in haste. He had an immediate obligation to fulfil with the Grand Final Parade being only minutes away. I said that we could not make an immediate assessment and that we would functionally test him after the parade to assess his power and ascertain if he would play.

Mick noted that Presti's hopes were evaporating quickly and could sense he was becoming emotional. It had been such a tense week; the pressure placed on AFL players in grand final week is enormous. Presti didn't need the added stress of querying his injury status only minutes before the parade was about to commence. The four of us in the room could feel the tension and empathised with him and felt his concerns. But there was an element of hope still alive.

To reassure Presti, Mick relayed a similar story about himself when he had missed the 1982 Grand Final through a shoulder injury.

Mick—1982 shoulder injury

I played every game for Richmond in 1982. It was during our semi-final clash with Carlton that I dislocated my shoulder.

Just before half time I tried to punch the ball to spoil a mark and slipped on the grass as I did so. I cannoned into my opponent's back with an outstretched arm and felt my right shoulder jerk backwards and a sensation of something ripping.

The team medicos strapped the shoulder during the break but as I was not feeling any great pain and was keen to play on, I returned to the field in the third term. In the first passage of play to come near the back pocket I was defending; again I went to punch the ball—a move I'd habitually done hundreds of times before—when my shoulder popped out. This time there was extreme pain.

I clearly remember sitting on the edge of the bath in the change rooms after our win—my teammates jubilant and excited around me—trying to come to grips with the fact that my injury might mean missing the grand final. (The finals system used then meant that winning the semi-final was an automatic path to the grand final.)

The body language of the doctors and coaches who enquired after my wellbeing suggested there was no hope.

Hopelessness is perhaps the worst emotion a human can feel. Without hope, there's nothing to gain, nothing to fight for. Without hope, there is simply nothing.

So I gave myself hope. I'd never felt hopelessness before—it was foreign to me—so I couldn't understand why others were trying to have a negative impact on me by suggesting I wouldn't get over my injury in time for the grand final.

I knew I had two weeks to convince not only the medical staff but also the coach that I would be right to play.

I received treatment religiously. I sought and followed all the rehabilitation advice I could gather from medical experts and teammates who had had the same injury. I worked so hard to recover that I had to sleep sitting up, as the throbbing pain in my shoulder was too acute when I lay down.

The first week was all entirely rehab work. By the second week I was back to full training. At least I was on the field with the rest of the team. This gave me more hope and I worked harder.

By the Thursday night before the Saturday grand final I had done enough to convince the selection committee that I deserved a fitness test. Up to this point I felt that I had been dismissed as a lost cause.

That night we trained as a team at the MCG in front of thousands of eager and animated Tigers supporters. The buzz within the club was building too, as we imagined celebrating another Premiership, having held the cup aloft just two years before.

From there we returned to Punt Road Oval, our usual training ground, where more fans, friends and family remained to cheer us on. Our coach, Francis Bourke (my teammate of many years—including the 1980 Premiership—and a man I have the utmost respect for both professionally and personally) put me through a searching fitness test.

To convince him of my readiness I needed to be pushed to the limit—and I was. I tackled hard; I took overhead marks and punched the ball with my 'bad' arm. No hope had shifted to a ray of hope.

By this time, my teammates had gathered on the sidelines to watch the final stages of the test. It was almost complete and the doctors were ready to give me the all-clear when I grabbed Francis' jumper with my right hand for a tackle, as my body weight shifted left.

It was an innocuous incident but my shoulder dislocated immediately and with it my hopes of competing in the grand final vanished. I was devastated.

I watched the game from the players' reserve bench at ground level, two days later. We lost to Carlton by 18 points.

I still think I could have played and been of use in the backline, though I respected the decision of the coach and the medical staff that my fitness was too risky to take into such an important game.

As I began my coaching career with Footscray just over a year later, I carried with me a lesson learnt from that experience: never dismiss hope. By at least giving a player hope, you give him (or the team or a family member) a reason to try. You give them the opportunity to live up to that hope.

In Round 21 of Collingwood's 2010 season, Alan Didak tore his pectoral muscle off the bone. It seemed to be a hopeless situation and Alan himself doubted whether he would be able to compete in the coming finals series.

David and I have an understanding: we never reveal our true concerns to an injured player and always lessen the time we believe it will take him to overcome his injury. We tell him he'll be back in three weeks instead of the five it may really be. By doing so, we give him hope and positivity and a target. If he makes it back in three weeks, fantastic. If he makes it back in five, we know he gave it his all trying to return in three.

After missing only one week, we told Alan that if he could play with pain, his natural ability and courage would get him through the finals series.

He not only played every final—including both grand finals—he excelled in them.

By being optimistic and working hard with the medical staff, Alan was able to manage his injury enough to take to the field each week. His efforts were rewarded by becoming a Premiership player. If we had taken away that spark of hope and displayed our fears to him, perhaps his season would have ended in Round 21, without celebration—as mine had 28 years earlier.

Hope is so simple to give and yet so powerful to receive. You may not always get the result you are hoping for, but by having hope in the first place, you try hard to achieve it. Just by doing that, you are on a path to personal success.

David—Simon Prestigiacomo and the 2010 grand final (continued)

Mick emphasised the importance of Presti showing true sportsmanship by remaining strong in front of the rest of the team, his family and the supporters. He stressed that if Presti became a blithering mess it would negatively affect the playing group. He could not emphasise enough the importance of Simon holding it together at this time despite the emotions that were running through him.

At the conclusion of the parade no one else was any the wiser about what had transpired in Gary's office less than an hour before. Presti, now in the company of Gary, Mick, rehab co-ordinator Justin Crow and me, was tested. I gave Presti a battery of tests that involved warming up and exercising to increase his range of motion so that a more rigorous, robust test could be conducted. Presti successfully completed the first stage of the testing. However, as the tests became more dynamic, we noted his diminished power and agility. At this stage his body language said it all. He felt he was going to be a withdrawal from the grand final team. I asked him if he thought he could get through the game the next day.

Many coaches have been fortunate enough to work with athletes who have shown a realistic perspective of ambition. Great athletes possess this and are to be respected. The words that Gary, Mick and I heard in the next instant echoed these qualities. Before us stood the most unselfish of men, a man of integrity who, despite his incredible desire to play in the pinnacle event for all footballers, the AFL grand final, had recognised and more impressively admitted that he was unfit to play. His words are still etched in all our minds: 'Give my position to Browny (Nathan Brown) as he is 100 per cent fit.'

As Albert Einstein so wisely recognised many years ago, true value comes from 'love and devotion to men'. Presti was selfless because he saw the bigger picture. He recognised that he was part of a team and to be a part of a team one must love one's sport, one's team and one's teammates above oneself. His love and devotion towards his team and his ability to view things objectively meant that he could see the bigger picture.

Nothing truly valuable arises from ambition or from a mere sense of duty; it stems rather from love and devotion towards men and towards objective things.

Albert Einstein

Presti missing the grand final
Luke Ball

I was so impressed with Presti and I was proud of what he did.

Scott Pendlebury

My initial thought was that it was selfless, and it really was the ultimate sacrifice in team sport that I've ever seen.

Character

Every year in November the national draft is conducted. All of the clubs in the AFL send key personnel from their recruiting and sometimes their football departments. In years gone by, players were recruited to clubs based on talent. They were watched in their allocated zones at junior level by recruiting scouts, who noted their statistics, performance, athleticism and skill. From this, some type of priority order was determined and clubs approached the potential player and invited him to join their team.

After discussions surrounding contracts and other arrangements, the player made his choice to accept an offer and became part of a new team and club. It was also assumed that the player would remain at that club for the remainder of his VFL (as it was then) career.

There was limited investigation of a player's personal traits. The player was assessed on his on-field performance alone.

Today, the recruitment of players has developed enormously. Before the November draft each year due diligence is performed on potential players. Potential players become aware that clubs have taken an interest in them and know that they have a chance of being recruited. In early October a training camp is conducted; potential recruits are invited to attend and perform specific tests on speed, endurance, agility, jumping and ball skills. As well as this, players are given medical screening and psychological assessments.

All this data provides valuable information in the selection of the new recruits for the following season's list. The most significant development over the last few years is the use of psychological profiling to gather information on a player's cognitive and emotional functioning. In other words, this has given clubs a greater insight into what makes the player tick. Complementing this, each player is interviewed by a panel of key personnel from each club. This allows clubs to gather even more information on the intangibles that the previous tests haven't shown.

David—Dale Thomas at the 2005 draft camp

Each year we travel to the Australian Institute of Sport in Canberra to meet the potential new recruits at the draft camp. In 2005, I noticed this happy kid with a big mop of blond hair who attempted every test with an extra spring in his step. He seemed like a ball of energy and I asked who he was. Derek Hine told me that he was a boy from Gippsland Power called Dale Thomas and that he had dominated in the recent TAC Cup Grand Final.

As I recollect, Mick, Derek, Simon Lloyd (our psychologist) and I were on the interview panel. The interview followed a familiar pattern. We asked general questions about football in an attempt to relax Dale at the start. As we progressed we delved deeper into his personal life and asked questions about his family, work, study and living arrangements. We further inquired about his aspirations, adversities and other experiences in life.

A positive quality that came across in the interview with Dale, apart from his happy demeanour, was his love for the game. He lit up the room with his energy and you couldn't help but be infected by his enthusiasm. But Dale's enthusiasm went beyond football. He was unashamedly proud of his mother and acknowledged her support and his love for her. He explained how, like many parents, she had taken him to all of his games and training sessions. Mick asked Dale about his father and he flippantly replied, 'I don't know! It's just my mum and my sister.'

The significant factor we all noticed was Dale's level of maturity and loyalty, his courage in recognising his mother's efforts of being a single mum and doing it all on her own. In that short space of time we all realised that before us was a young man of character. Although making the AFL was obviously his big dream, he could still acknowledge his mother's contribution to his life and that she was one of the reasons he was sitting in that room talking to us. And he was prepared to acknowledge it publicly. It left a lasting impression on me.

Dale continues to demonstrate this strength of character. He happily goes out into the community and gives to others. Further confirmation of his character is demonstrated by his loyalty to his teammates and the courage and commitment with which he plays the game. Interestingly, not one of the tests at that draft camp identified the most significant trait that Dale possesses: character.

Dale Thomas—2005 draft camp interview

I was in awe being in the room with Mick and having him interviewing me. I wanted to say the right things, but I kept my answers totally honest. I really wanted to leave an impression.

Andy Krakouer—Recruited to Collingwood

I wanted to make sure I did the right things and made a positive impression.

When you watch a player on the field it's sometimes difficult to get a handle on his true character. Alan Didak's generous gesture for the small orphanage in South Africa and Simon Prestigiacomo's on grand final eve both showed examples of character, yet neither action was known to the public at the time.

Many characters make up a football club; some stand out more than others for different qualities and reasons. It is those special individuals who bind a group or lead a pack that impress the most, such as James Clement and Chris Mainwaring.

> *A person's true character is revealed by what he does when no one is watching.*
>
> Anonymous

Mick—Character
James Clement

At the end of the 2000 season during trade week we traded draft picks 8 and 39 for two Fremantle Dockers players. They were James Clement and Brodie Holland.

The Fremantle hierarchy had labelled Jimmy 'soft'. He was tall (190 centimetres) well-built (94 kilograms at playing weight) and he could play at either end of the ground. However, the Dockers put him up for trade because they believed he wasn't hard enough in the trenches. (Admittedly we had Freo over a barrel as they desperately needed our first-round pick to get Peter Bell from North Melbourne.)

In my time at the West Coast Eagles I had seen Jimmy develop from an under-18 player to an AFL player with a promising career. To my eye, he lacked confidence in his own abilities. Because he could play anywhere, he was used everywhere. However, if he didn't succeed in the different roles each week, it was felt that he couldn't master one position. This eroded his confidence. Although he had enormous ability, by his final year at Fremantle his confidence had deteriorated to a point that his performance was affected and he managed only eight games for the season, spending most of the year with his WAFL club, South Fremantle.

This is not softness or weakness; this is confusion and lack of direction.

One thing Fremantle did convey about Jimmy was that he was a fantastic bloke. He had great character, he was an upstanding citizen and everyone at the club liked and admired him. Our due diligence supported this entirely.

It was a no-brainer, then, that we wanted him at Collingwood. He had a strong character, intelligence, strength, height and pace and would fit perfectly into our backline. With a consistent role to play, we felt he would thrive.

He made his Magpie debut in Round 3 of the 2001 season and went on to play 20 sound games that year. Within a short time he became a natural leader at the club and was officially named vice-captain in 2004.

Off the field, Jimmy is an exceptional husband to Jeanne and father to Annabelle and Thomas. During his time at Collingwood, premature births and the illness of family members created even more responsibility for him and definitely added to the weight on his shoulders.

As a coach, I always like to know roughly what's going on in a player's personal life. I don't need all the details (that's their business) but it helps to know if things are tough, for example, so I can take it into consideration when assessing the player's on-field contributions. Not everyone will play an outstanding game week in, week out. As humans, they will be affected by what's happening in their off-field lives and coaches (and leaders) need to understand, address and support this.

Jimmy never complained. I remember in a practice match one year, Jimmy took a high hit and suffered a severe eye injury. The club doctors said he was close to having the eyeball dislodged from the socket (such an injury is usually only associated with a car accident or similar). And yet Jimmy downplayed the gravity of the situation, saying, 'I'm okay.' If I hadn't received some information from other parties (his close friends), I wouldn't have known what was happening in his life away from the club. He had more to contend with than most, yet he remained stoic and totally in charge of every situation on and off the field at the club.

When Jimmy came to my home and knocked on my front door in September 2007, I knew he had something important to tell me. He was retiring at 31 years of age after 230 games (146 at Collingwood) and still at the top of his game.

I am a self-professed admirer of James Clement. As a coach I thought he was retiring too early (and I didn't want to lose him from the team) but as a person I knew he needed to retire for his family's sake. His great character once again struck me and my admiration for him grew further.

As a two-time Copeland Trophy winner and twice All Australian team member, Jimmy had succeeded at the highest level.

His focus, drive and wholehearted commitment to the team put him at a level above most. Jimmy didn't take prisoners. He wouldn't accept complaints and excuses from his teammates. They all admired and respected him for this tough approach.

He would have been captain of the Collingwood Football Club if not for his retirement. Scott Burns was named captain on Nathan Buckley's departure and he was a good leader. But I know Jimmy would have held that post and also done an exceptional job.

It wasn't meant to be and now, looking back, I'm glad that he was able to finish football with something in the cup rather than nothing at all. I still remember watching Richmond great Royce Hart walking slowly around the boundary, injured in his final game of his last season, having continued for one year too many. It has always stuck in my mind and taught me that getting out on top is better than staying too long.

It turned out that James' decision was the best one for him and his family and I congratulate him for having the courage to end his football career when he needed to.

Chris Mainwaring

Mainy was a lovable rogue. He was a member of the West Coast Eagles' inaugural squad, but I met Mainy when I first began at the club at the end of 1989. He was on the verge of turning 24, bleary-eyed and clearly affected by a late night out. I would come to learn that Chris not only worked hard, but played hard too.

I tend to get angry and disappointed by people who don't try to get the best out of themselves, but I can assure you I had no need to feel that way about Mainy. He was an enigma who left no stone unturned to be his best. He had to train (and did so) at an exceptional level to balance his off-field life.

Chris played 201 games for the Eagles (including two Premierships) and was named in their Team of the Decade in 1996 as well as earning All Australian selection in 1991 and 1996. His leap for joy on the siren—with a broken ankle—at the '92 grand final is an image that represents well the person that he was.

His effervescent enthusiasm and infectious grin made it difficult to feel anything but love for him. His professionalism on the track may have belied what his life was like off it, but it didn't change your opinion of him—that he was an amazing character.

Without going into the details surrounding his death, the hard and fast pace at which he lived his life meant it was no great surprise that his life was cut short. However, it was still a shock when it happened and, I believe, one of life's great tragedies. It took me a long time to get over it.

Mick—Anthony Rocca: The truths

Anthony possessed wonderful qualities as a footballer. He had an acute awareness of football strategies, explosive athletic qualities and a massive heart for the contest. He was a match-winner and a great team man full of character. He tried to do everything right by the team and club. The falsehoods spread about him being unfit, having no endurance, being slow, lazy and letting the team down in big games were often media-driven—nothing could be further from the truth. Anthony nearly singlehandedly won the 2002 grand final against one of the great teams of recent AFL history. I am privileged to have had him as a player and now as a colleague and friend.

In sports people, having character can imply a variety of attributes that give the person credibility and durability. Qualities and virtues such as these men displayed—of loyalty, honesty and courage—reflect some features of character. It is in times of adversity and high pressure—such as the 2010 grand finals—that character is truly tested.

CHAPTER 8

OVERCOMING SETBACKS AND ADVERSITY

Of all the things that people experience in their lives, the most challenging and revealing of character are setbacks and adversity. How often have you looked at someone's unfortunate situation and been grateful that you're not suffering the same plight as them? But some time down the track everyone faces their own big problems; it's often just a matter of time.

David—Tom Hunter's challenge

It was an apparently innocuous incident in the first quarter of the 2011 NAB Cup against the West Coast Eagles at Subiaco that caused second-year rookie Tom Hunter to leave the field with a neck injury. The medicos examined him and quickly announced that he was out for the rest of the game. Tom was experiencing unusual sensations in both arms and was aware that something wasn't right. We could see a look of worry on his face.

He was taken down to the rooms for further assessment and his neck was immobilised. An ambulance was called to take him to the Royal Perth Hospital. The injury turned out to be quite severe and he had to remain in hospital for a few days before he was given the all-clear to fly home wearing a neck brace. On his return to Melbourne he was sent to various specialists for further examination. The players kept asking how he was and what his future held. The immediate diagnosis was that he was not allowed to play for the next few weeks. Other than that, little was known.

The process of collating the specialists' reports took some time and this in itself was a concern. Things were not looking too promising for Tom, but he always kept a glimmer of hope that he might return to training and playing. Finally the specialists provided their assessment and a meeting was arranged with Tom, his parents, Geoff Walsh, Tony Page (the doctor), David Stiff (the high-performance manager) and me.

Walshy chaired the meeting and outlined Tom's situation clearly and empathetically. He talked about how, as a club, we held a duty of care to his health and wellbeing and said that the specialists' reports indicated that any further involvement in contact sport could be catastrophic. Tony elaborated and clarified the situation further, outlining the risks involved. He reassured Tom that he could continue to live a healthy life, but only if he refrained from playing contact sport—in other words, football. The decision of playing contact sports in the future really lay with Tom, but as far as his position on the team went, the Collingwood management were not going to allow him to continue to play at their club.

You could see the distress on his face; tears were welling up in his eyes. Although he secretly may have known what the message from Walshy was going to be, he had held the hope that he might be able to play again. Walshy asked him what his thoughts were and Tom said that he realised that he could not continue. He had a quiver in his voice and then broke down crying. All of us in the room felt his distress and shared it. His parents were experiencing all his pain with him; it showed on their faces. On one hand, he was being told shattering news and yet on the other, he was being given another chance at a life with a healthy future.

After gathering his thoughts and digesting the news Tom was adamant that he wanted to remain a part of the team. He realised, of course, that he could not play again, but he could be involved in some capacity. He asked if he could stay at the club and train to some degree with the rest of the boys. We all felt moved by this gesture in his time of adversity. Although he must have been devastated knowing his dream was over, he was selfless and thought about the rest of his teammates.

Tom Hunter—Injury

Initially I was devastated and frustrated. Being told that I wasn't able to play anymore when I couldn't even feel any pain in my neck made it worse. All the hours of hard work that I'd put in—my dream of playing AFL just came to a stop. I realised the situation I was in, but emotionally it was huge to deal with and a massive challenge for me. Being a runner for the team now means a lot to me; I feel that now I can be useful for the group and I want to support them. My family, my girlfriend and my club have been there for me, which helps enormously. I am so appreciative. I know you can't control certain things in your life but we do have a choice about how we respond.

Setback versus adversity

A s*etback* is often seen as a single event that requires immediate action, while *adversity* is usually ongoing and needs to be addressed with continuous and steady action. This may be easier to understand if you compare an injury to an illness. A setback could be a broken leg, which may require surgery and immediate treatment for it to heal, while adversity could be a serious illness that requires ongoing regular treatment with no guarantee of a cure.

Adversity is usually accompanied by feelings of anxiety, stress, disappointment and fear. But if it is accompanied by hopelessness then the impact is even more significant, and can grow to utter despair, feeling that there is no chance, nothing to look forward to and that something has ended, permanently. It's true that setbacks and adversity do signal the end of something—but not always permanently. In sport, if a player suffers a rupture of their anterior cruciate ligament (ACL) and requires a knee reconstruction, it may signal the end of that particular season, but it does not necessarily signal the end of their career.

David—Tarkyn Lockyer's knee reconstruction

In 2002, Tarkyn Lockyer played in the grand final, narrowly missing out against the Brisbane Lions. In early 2003 he had had a fantastic preseason, but in Round 3 misfortune cruelly struck in the form of a ruptured ACL, forcing a knee reconstruction.

After successful surgery he began his rehabilitation with me. In the first six weeks he had the quickest recovery of any player I have worked with and was ahead of schedule. The likelihood of him playing in the latter part of the season was very feasible. This was an exciting prospect since Collingwood was going to get finals action again.

While he was rehabilitating, Tarkyn was able to use his setback to focus on other areas of his fitness, such as strength, work tolerance and professionalism to take his mind off his knee. He was on track to play in the latter rounds of the season. He met all the criteria and fitness assessments to resume full training.

But Tarkyn was faced with another setback. Before he was able to resume his position in the team, he developed a fracture in his foot. His hopes of playing in the finals were gone and he knew he had to face the arduous task of putting the season behind him and starting his rehab again. He went on and faced the task ahead of him with conviction and resumed playing again in the 2004 season.

Although he never played in a grand final again, he finished his career with 227 games under his belt and now is coaching Collingwood's VFL team. His injuries were setbacks, but not career-ending.

Tarkyn Lockyer—Overcoming injury

I was still hurting from not winning the 2002 grand final and doing my knee in 2003 just topped it off. I was very anxious going into the surgery; my heart rate was high, my blood pressure was up. I had doubt. I didn't know whether I'd come back to my normal self. This is what got my 'driving force' going; I wanted to push myself to prove I could get better. I changed my mindset to work on becoming a better footballer and a stronger person. I wanted to raise the bar and I was never scared of having a go. Before I did my knee I would question my capabilities. But overcoming this setback gave me the ability to realise that you can only control what you can control. So I just kept reloading and developed faith in myself and the people around me.

Mick—Tarkyn Lockyer

Knee injuries have a huge impact on athletes. It is not just the physical pain, but also the psychological barrier that can prolong recovery and the time it takes to get back to action. They don't remember the pain of the injury the moment it was sustained; they remember the type of injury they suffered. On returning, most athletes are too cautious, worrying about it happening again.

As we've seen, it was such an accomplishment when Tarkyn Lockyer was ready to return in almost half the time initially diagnosed. Tarkyn was a young man with an incredible desire to play football—that's why the club rookie-listed him in the first place. After recovering from his anterior cruciate ligament surgery, Tarks had a further setback when he broke a bone in his foot and required another operation.

He came back like there was no tomorrow, in record time. His mental strength and determination was such that he got straight back into the rhythm of things without missing a beat. He was back on the field, resuming his role in the leadership group and enjoying footy once again.

For Tarkyn, a knee injury had merely been an inconvenience. There was a never a question that it could be career-threatening, because he wouldn't let that option enter his mind. He did what he had to do to return to what he loved—playing football.

Wake-up calls

Setbacks and adversity should be recognised for what they really are: wake-up calls. They jolt us out of our slumber and eliminate complacency. Who would have thought that the 2010 grand final would end up a draw? Who would have thought that teams would have to repeat their grand final preparation and play again the following week? One single event gave both clubs probably their greatest wake-up call for quite some time.

Adversity and setbacks can be pretty difficult to accept. We often choose to resist them and so do not recognise them for what they really are. Players who are coming to the end of their careers can be loath to face the prospects of not playing their beloved sport anymore—the thing that gave them such joy is coming to an end. But endings are inevitable; all things end! The length and timing of them may vary, but at some point they finish. Careers in all fields only have a certain life span, businesses could go bankrupt, people retire due to age, prospects of a more exciting job can cause an exit from one place of employment to another, but end they do.

Paul Licuria—On retiring

I was extremely disappointed . . . I knew it was coming, but I was trying to hold on to my dreams for just a bit longer. There wasn't a day that went by that I didn't think of the grand final losses, particularly working in the football environment. Playing a role in the grand final of 2010 did help heal the pain.

In other areas of life, such as relationships, endings can occur for myriad reasons. When you're at school, relationships change due to people growing up and developing new interests. Relationships may not survive due to a physical move to another city or state. Partnerships may not survive for a variety of reasons, including poor communication, financial issues or, more permanently, death. Endings are inevitable.

Everything has an end.

Geoffrey Chaucer

Mick—Overcoming my own adversity

Everyone has a start and an end point; this is no truer than for the career of an AFL footballer.

When he begins, the young AFL footballer is starry-eyed and excited about the future. He can sense his dream becoming reality and he wants to jump straight into it.

By his mid-20s, the footballer is well-established within the ranks of AFL players. He has achieved his vision of playing footy at an elite level and perhaps, if he's lucky, he's already had success, be it personal or team triumph. He still has a desire to play on.

By 30, the footballer has virtually reached his peak. His career is not over—maybe not for some years—but at this age he starts to feel vulnerable. This is when he needs to begin looking beyond football, to a life outside of the game. But many don't—the thought of it all ending is too frightening.

When someone is scared or faced with a tough situation—too tough, sometimes, to contemplate overcoming it—they can tend to stand still. This will never fix the problem. It's in times of adversity that we need to stand up and keep moving. It is in this moment that we must do what has to be done to get through the rough patch (and this is usually all it is), to advance beyond the difficulty and progress.

I knew my parents were old and frail and yet when they died it still came as a shock. My father had cancer. We were told it was critical and that it would take his life. The speed at which that happened, though, took me by surprise. He passed away on 13 August 2007—a Monday.

Collingwood was playing on the Friday—my birthday, 17 August—against Melbourne at the MCG.

I was in a zombie-like state and many had suggested that I stay out of the coaches' box that week and give myself time to grieve. The grieving would continue well past that week, as would the thought that my father would have wanted me to coach.

Dad loved football and introduced me to the game when I was a boy. Together with my mother he attended most of the matches that I played in and then coached throughout my career. It was a joy in their life to support and barrack for me. Football was close to religion for them.

So for me it was a simple decision to take my usual seat in the box that Friday night and coach the match. Collingwood beat the Demons by 11 points. I can tell you the result now because I can check it in the history books, though at the time I wouldn't even have been able to tell you which team we played. I was numb but had control of my position.

Somehow the courage my father had shown throughout his life and then in his death gave me the strength to fulfil my role as coach that week. I won't deny it was one of the toughest things I have had to do in my career, nor will I claim I didn't shed a tear after the game, but I did what I had to do and did it to the best of my ability.

Two years later, almost to the day, I lost my mother to cancer. Again it was expected, but quick, and once again it was a shock.

In our final conversation at the hospice she said something I will never forget: 'Michael I worry about you.' When I asked her why she said, 'I worry about the pressures on you as a coach.'

Although she was dying, my mother was concerned for my welfare in this game we had dedicated so much of our lives to. For this and for her, I yet again coached a game that same week. She passed away on Tuesday 18 August and we defeated Sydney at the MCG the following Sunday. She would have wanted it that way.

Sometimes we do things in life we don't necessarily want to through obligation, guilt or maybe respect. Sometimes we don't do things we should because of fear, neglect or indifference.

Adversity comes in many forms, in various situations, for individuals and for groups. As testing as these times can be, this is exactly what they are—a test. Do what you have to do to pass and you will see that adversity is just a hurdle to jump, a challenge to overcome. Adversity will make you stronger— it will help you to do things better and to achieve things you may never have thought possible. It is the times when we stand up under pressure and put all else aside to complete a task that we will remember and be remembered for.

Mick—Leon Davis

Leon Davis has been much maligned in the 12 years he has played at Collingwood and yet he, of all people, should be applauded for what he has achieved in difficult circumstances.

Leaving behind a large but very close family in remote Western Australia, 18-year-old Leon had to overcome severe shyness to travel on his own to Melbourne and make a home for himself there. He had to do this to play football at the highest level.

It was an enormous adjustment for Leon to undertake, dealing with a change of not only environment but culture as well. We made it our mission to make him feel as welcome and comfortable as possible at the Magpies. He overcame the mental challenge of such a big move with what seemed to be relative ease in the end and debuted for the Pies in Round 1, 2000.

He has since become the first Indigenous player to reach 100 and then 200 games for Collingwood, a massive accomplishment and one he should be very proud of. By rewriting the history books, Leon changed the landscape of the club forever and for the better.

People have questioned his ability to produce the type of football we are used to seeing from 'Neon Leon' in big games. Yes, he has had some below-average games in finals, but so have many others. He has also played some brilliant football at times when we needed it the most.

Leon has overcome many negative influences and challenges to be the best as often as he could.

Mick—Travelling Eagles

In my first year in charge of the West Coast Eagles, 1990, we finished third for the season and competed in the finals—a good result after finishing eleventh the previous season.

Being a non-Victorian team, the travel demands were heavy. Everyone had to fly across the country for matches, sometimes two and three weeks in a row. This got to a ridiculous level by the end of the season when we had to travel for six weeks straight.

In Round 21 we had to take two flights to get us from Perth to the Gold Coast to play Brisbane at Carrara Stadium. We won by 41 points.

In Round 22 we played Geelong at their home ground, Kardinia Park. This meant a flight to Melbourne then a long bus trip down the highway. We won the game by seven points.

It was finals next, so more travelling was involved. Under AFL rules (which have since been updated), we couldn't have a finals game at our home ground, Subiaco Oval.

We drew with Collingwood in the first qualifying final at Waverley Park and had to return to Victoria the following week to play the game all over again. We were thumped, 19.12 (126) to 9.13 (67).

So we regrouped our forces for another finals assault. No one thought we would survive this game, our fifth week on the road. We played Melbourne, who were in good form, at Waverley Park in the semi-final and defeated them by 30 points.

The week of the preliminary final there was an airline strike. In the end, to fly our entire team and staff from Western Australia to Melbourne, we had to commute with another sporting team, the NBL's Perth Wildcats, on a chartered flight. Cramming into the back of the aircraft (to allow the taller basket-ballers more leg room in the front of the plane) we stopped in Kalgoorlie and then Mildura before finally reaching Melbourne after many hours in the air.

By now the players were feeling both mentally and physically drained. This is not an excuse, merely an honest observation. For our sixth game away we faced Essendon at the MCG and got thrashed. I was not really surprised by the result, just very disappointed.

As difficult and trying as the travel that year was—six weeks straight is unheard of in world elite sport—I feel now that it galvanised and bonded us as a group and set us up for success in the two years that followed. We made the 1991 grand final (though we lost to Hawthorn) and won the 1992 Premiership (against Geelong). Our previous hardship had taught us how to travel better and more efficiently and what had to be done to repeatedly win away from home.

We took the AFL cup out of Victoria for the first time since the game's inception and, in a sense, completed the creation of a truly national competition.

Trevor Nisbett, CEO of the West Coast Eagles—Mick's defining moment

In 1990 we played six away games on the trot. It was challenging and demanding for the group. Mick had a significant impact on the group and turned this experience into a positive one. It developed the group's resilience and the culture of the club.

That which does not kill us makes us stronger.

Friedrich Nietzsche

Hopelessness can be all-consuming. It can engulf and cloud all rational thought. We can feel isolated and alone, like we are the only one suffering. Thoughts abound that no one else understands how we are feeling and what we are going through. We can feel like victims, that it is all just too unfair.

Chris Dawes—Mt Humphreys

The hardest session is when you are on your own; it's so lonely. Mt Humphreys was brutal. I don't know whether I was sweating or crying. I felt brain-dead. I was asking myself, 'What am I doing here?' I even briefly wished I could trip on a rock and break my ankle so I could stop. Fifteen minutes later I was so rapt that I'd done it.

There's a point at which we must take stock. Sometimes we have to force ourselves to do it, but we must stop and make a choice. For it is not about the situation at all. It is not what has happened to us that is important, but how we respond. Will we react negatively or positively? Which path will we go down?

What would have happened if Collingwood had decided to take the view after the drawn grand final that it was unfair? What might have taken place the next week if the club had thought that there was no hope? Or how unfair it was that there had been a draw when they had worked so hard to get to the grand final? It's more than likely that the effect would have been a negative one and the final result not in our favour. Setbacks and adversity must be embraced and, in fact, encouraged, for it is in these times that we experience our greatest growth.

Tarkyn Lockyer—Missing the drawn grand final

Missing the grand final was the worst experience I have had. I knew I was very close to being selected, but it didn't go my way. The thing that gets me through is that I left no stone unturned and I did everything possible; I wasn't going to die wondering. I was so rapt to see the boys win the flag. It was a great reward for all the work they had put in over the years, altitude training camps and the constant hard grind of perseverance.

Ben Reid—World of pain

So often I have been in a world of pain, but once I've done the hard work and accomplished the task, I feel stronger in myself.

World War II survivor and psychiatrist Victor Frankl, author of *Man's Search for Meaning*, suffered all manner of adversity and atrocities while in a German concentration camp. Yet the firm belief he held during the most horrendous of circumstances was that surviving was all about one's attitude to one's situation: 'When we are no longer able to change a situation—we are challenged to change ourselves.'

Ben Reid—Changing his ways

When I started I didn't know how hard I could really push myself. My goal was to play one AFL game. I had doubts in my second year whether I was going to make it. I had injury frustrations. My mates were playing and I was on the side watching. I willed myself to get there, I worked hard in the gym with Butters, I watched others who were great and then I started to change my ways.

Staying calm

After the initial feelings of anxiety and disappointment, it's common for one to feel denial or anger. Once there has been an acceptance of the situation, there's room to embrace it and move forward. If you can stay calm, you can review old methods and patterns in your life, consider how others have handled similar situations and make room for new methods and patterns.

Paul Licuria—Drawn grand final

There was a lot of chaos and I was intrigued to watch what was going on. There were so many people who wanted to get involved. I noticed that a few people panicked, but I saw Mick and Butters steadying the ship. They put structure back into the system again.

In the discussion that took place on the ground immediately after the siren of the first grand final in 2010, calmness and positivity were essential, particularly with players hovering around. Lessons were taken from others who had been in the same situation, such as the draw of 1977, where North Melbourne had shared the evening with their families, and positivity was evident in the speeches that evening at Collingwood's post-match dinner. By far the most important quality in facing adversity and hardship is sheer determination. It must be addressed for it will not abate until it is looked directly in the eye and faced head-on.

David—Nick's story

'Hi Mick,' I said.

'G'day Butters, how're you going?' Mick asked in reply.

'I'm not too good. Nick has taken his life.' I answered. First there was silence and then from the other end of the phone I heard, 'Oh Butters, oh mate, I'm so sorry.'

It was Friday 27 February 2009 and I was about to ride to work when I noticed my bike had a puncture, which delayed me. As I was repairing it I heard my wife, Maria, scream out my name and call me to come quickly. Maria is a very calm person so I knew straight away that something terrible had happened. I sprinted inside. What we had feared for many years had happened. My eldest son, Nicholas, had taken his life. What we fought so hard against for many years had finally beaten us. My initial reaction was total devastation. I'd lost my boy. Maria was sobbing desolately and I held her.

As a young boy Nick had been gifted in so many ways. He had a musical talent that people spend years striving for and still never achieve. Nick was the life of the party and could light up a room. People often commented on how, even as a little boy, he could leave a lasting impression—sometimes with his cheeky antics, but usually because he had an incredible ability to make you feel so good about yourself. However, under this happy demeanour was a young man with his fair share of struggles who had been fighting fiercely to overcome them. I had the greatest admiration for his courage. But sometimes the body and mind have just had enough and for Nick this time had come. We had tried to understand the suffering that he bore, but as someone once said, you never know what someone else is going through until you walk a mile in their shoes.

As we were making the necessary phone calls, sharing the tragic news with our family and friends, people started arriving at our home. After my phone call to Mick, he and Geoff Walsh arrived in what appeared to be no time at all. They were so quick that our other children had not even arrived home and been told the sad news yet.

Our emotions were raw and uncontrollable and so our response to people was natural and vulnerable. We were in a cloud and clarity of thought was completely nonexistent. But we knew that, as parents, we had to dig deep and find some form of control, because we had three other children who needed us to tell them what had happened. They needed to be told by Maria and me.

Family members had gone to collect our children from their various schools and bring them home to us. Maria and I asked them not to tell them why they were being picked up. I remember my eldest brother, Paul, arriving in the driveway with our second-youngest child, Dylan. Dylan was a fresh-faced, upbeat 12-year-old kid who had not been told any tragic news before. I was dreading breaking the news to him as he idolised his oldest brother. I was hurting so very deeply and I just didn't want to pass on this terrible news to my children, which I knew would bring such unbearable pain.

Initially I wanted to pass the buck to my brother and get him to do it. Then I could let go of the responsibility and sink deeper into the abyss I had fallen into. Instinctively, as parents, we want to protect our children, but being a responsible parent includes helping them confront any event or challenge that they may encounter, and here we were facing one. I knew that I had to face it too and be the one to tell him, but I also did not want Dylan to feel the pain that I knew was going to change him forever. To be the bearer of bad news to a loved one, particularly your child, is probably one of the worst experiences you'll ever have to go through. But I went ahead and faced my responsibility and etched on my memory is the vision of his pain as he heard the news.

You never know how things will unfold in circumstances like this. And you never know who will support you until the time comes. Nick's younger sister, Emily, showed strength and leadership, taking on a nurturing role with her younger siblings; earlier she'd loved and helped Nick through difficult times.

Nick was the eldest of our four children; Emily, Dylan and then Bronte followed him. I have so many happy memories of him—we talked a lot about football, learnt to surf together, shared family holidays and all the Christmases and birthdays . . . so many happy occasions. I also remember his struggles and difficulties and trying to help him see his own worth as well as his value in this world.

Although there were some times when we felt hopelessness, a little ray of light would always shine from somewhere, be it his relationship with his family and friends or his music. I remember how, on many occasions, people would be at our house—sometimes Collingwood players—and Nick would entertain them with singing, playing his guitar or piano. One fun memory I have was a jam session in our back room with some former players—Steve McKee, Mark McGough and Brodie Holland. As they bashed away at their instruments, Nick was always encouraging, even if they were out of tune or off-key. And at Emily's eighteenth birthday party he was obliging and played for the Shaw brothers (Rhys and Heath) as well as Ben Johnson (Johnno) as they belted out some tunes. Johnno was requesting love songs and admitted to being a fan of Sunday night's 'Love Song Dedications' on the radio, much to everyone else's amusement.

The days following Nick's death were a blur. We had family, friends, players, staff and neighbours all coming through the house to express their condolences but also, more importantly, their support and love. We were fed, cared for and listened to. We were never alone in our pain; the several hundred people who walked through our doors over the next few weeks were also suffering.

On one particular day, just before Nick's funeral, ten to twenty players from the club came to visit us. Young men who I had led, who looked up to me due to my seniority and age, were comforting me. In my role at the club it was usually me who was supporting them for whatever reason; now the shoe was on the other foot.

I remember Alan Didak approaching me, not knowing what to say and then he just put his arms around me and embraced me as we both sobbed. Alan had been to see Nick's band play on numerous occasions. He had supported his music and was even working on getting Nick's band a record deal. He demonstrated an empathy that was reflective of so many people. I also recall Neil Balme coming into our home—as he had on many other occasions, with the view to helping us—and breaking down. He uttered through his tears, 'I came here to support you and look at me!' We both laughed at how hopeless we were.

Unbeknown to us at the time, Nick's death had not only rocked his family and friends, it had also rocked the community. All these gestures of support showed us that Nick and our family were very much loved and supported and that gave us strength and hope. The funeral arrived and we were able to cope and turn it into a celebration of his life.

As I was delivering his eulogy, I looked out at the sea of faces in the jam-packed church and saw so many people who had been a part of my life, ranging from when I was a young boy to the present day. This gave me the strength to go on. It wasn't until we walked out of the church and we saw the streets lined with people that we realised just how many people had come to support us; many had flown in from interstate. We were able to move through the occasion with the knowledge that it would pass and it was made easier because of all the people around us and the strength and love they gave us.

A few days after the funeral I woke up to the sound of movement in Dylan's room. When I checked the clock I saw it was six-thirty. I went and asked him what he was doing and he told me he was getting ready for school. This taught me so much. I thought that if he could get himself up and face the day, so could I. We knew that, with little steps, things were going to be normal again—a different normal—but normal again they'd be.

Facing adversity is not easy. Who's to judge what is the right or wrong way to resolve and deal with the struggles you are confronted with? Very often, when adversity is presented to you, you can be sure it's when you were least expecting it. No person's adversity should be compared or measured with another's. As individuals we experience pain differently; we all have different coping strategies. So something that may seem small to one person can be enormous to another. What is important is how you choose to deal with it. You can be certain that the support of others strengthens your resolve to overcome the struggles you may encounter.

David—Harry O'Brien's father

After Nick's funeral the family was talking about the people who had attended. One of my children asked if Harry had been there. I told them that I had had a phone call from him. He'd had to fly back to Perth because his father was missing. We were all very concerned.

We reminisced about the time when Harry, as a new recruit, had come over to our house and played the guitar with Nick. I had invited him over to dinner because he had recently relocated from Perth and it was obvious he was missing his family. Unlike the other 'wannabe musos' who had come to our house from the club, Harry could actually play and sing well. He sang a song from the country where he was born, Brazil, which was entertaining and moving. I recall him saying how he enjoyed sharing the evening with our family as it reminded him of his own family back in Perth.

Little did we know that night that some years down the track we would both endure similar adversity in a short space of time. Shortly after this reminiscing, it was confirmed that Harry's father had also taken his own life. From my own experience, which was so fresh in my mind, I could only imagine the pain he and his family were going through. I rang him and we both could feel each other's pain. He apologised for not attending Nick's funeral. I replied, 'Don't be silly, your family needed you and they are going to need you for some time to come.'

Harry's situation was different to mine in that he and his family were living in different states. The club supported Harry and gave him as much time as he needed because they knew he would be expected to take on certain responsibilities now that his father had gone. Harry remained there and helped his family during those early days, but he also acknowledged that he had a responsibility to his teammates and the club. He returned to Melbourne and was ready to play the first game of the season.

This may seem a reasonable time to get things in order, but grief can't be hurried. Harry would have been experiencing the most terrible anguish being away from his family. He tried to overcome his adversity by resuming his normal routine, despite his grief. I had the greatest admiration for him.

Curbing doubts

Although it is often others who help us overcome our challenges, we also must take control of our own situation. In times of adversity our self-belief is tested. We question ourselves and sometimes even question things or areas where we have been successful in the past. A player may have to go through a second shoulder reconstruction and, because he's frustrated about possibly missing the rest of the season, he doubts his ability to resume playing at his previous standard. This player coped very successfully with his rehabilitation program from the first shoulder operation. But because it happened twice, the seeds of self-doubt enter his thoughts like unwelcome visitors. Sometimes doubts come from others and we use this as an excuse to continue doubting ourselves.

The key to self-belief is to curb your doubts. To do this you must deliberately and consciously rebuild your positive self-belief by altering your behaviour and your thoughts. That self-doubting inner voice must be replaced with positive self-talk. You should consciously and intentionally repeat positive thoughts until they become habitual and you start to believe yourself. Then your self-belief grows and those around you start to believe in you more. You develop confidence in your ability and possibilities.

Scott Pendlebury—Mt Humphreys

The cold, the uneven footing, the extremity and the mental challenge of our climb up Humphreys Peak were so testing. I gained so much confidence and belief from doing that altitude training and I draw upon that frequently in hard training sessions, but also, more importantly, during games when it gets tough.

Focussing on successful challenges and accomplishments will make room for positive self-talk and a good self-image. By reflecting back on challenging times we can develop our confidence. Just like the player on his second shoulder reconstruction—with the right mindset his confidence will grow because he tells himself he has done this before, he has returned to full capacity before, so he can do it again.

Sometimes, however, we are faced with new and unexpected experiences. In these times it can help to think back on other times when we have approached and overcome difficulties. We gain confidence from knowing that we have overcome difficulty in the past and can draw on these experiences to tackle new challenges and difficulties.

David—Andrew Krakouer

A few weeks after the 2010 grand final, Derek Hine asked me if I could catch up with a new recruit, Andy Krakouer, over in Perth. Before I left, Derek gave me his game edits from the 2010 grand final, in which he had played with the Swan Districts Football Club. I knew he'd played over a hundred games with Richmond prior to this and had been away from the AFL for a few years, so I asked Derek what type of player he was. Without giving much away he said,

'Just watch his game, Butters and let me know what you think.' Derek has an uncanny ability to pick talent from obscure places and often sees what others don't, so I was looking forward to watching Andy play.

Before I left Melbourne I watched the footage of the 2010 grand final between Swan Districts and Claremont. Andy's outstanding display saw him dominate the game. He was clearly best-on-ground in the WAFL grand final and won the Simpson Medal for the best player on the field. He had 40 possessions and kicked 4 goals. His last goal, in the dying minutes of the game, put his team in front to snatch victory. It was the most impressive individual grand final game I've seen. His finesse, creativity and hard work were outstanding.

A few days later I flew over and met him. Andy was unable to fly over to Melbourne due to his parole obligations in Western Australia. In 2008 he had been jailed after an assault charge, following an incident that had occurred in 2006. I was curious to meet the young man who could play such an impressive game of football after being away from playing for some time in what must have been a challenging environment, to say the least.

My job when meeting Andy was to assess where he was at and prescribe a short-term fitness regime for him to follow until he was able to get permission to relocate and commence training with Collingwood. Andy met me at the airport. My initial impression was that he was a polite, articulate and quietly spoken man. I referred to his grand final performance and congratulated him on his efforts. He was quick to dismiss this and take the attention away from himself. He acknowledged his teammates and his coach. He drove me to the Swan Districts FC in Bassendean and proudly showed me around the club. He was keen to introduce me to one of his mentors, Peter Matera, a former West Coast Eagles champion.

Andy and I sat down and had a chat. I explained the training set-up at Collingwood and how he would be expected to fit into this. We discussed elements of our program, including altitude training, and I expressed the hope that he would be able to attend the forthcoming camp in Arizona. Noticing that he was carrying some unnecessary kilos, I suggested that he would need to immediately address his dietary habits to change his body composition. Andy was aware that, given Collingwood's recent success, he would have to commit to training at an elite level and do everything exceptionally well to earn himself a spot in the team.

Because of what Andy had been through over the last few years, I wanted to show him that the club would offer as much support as we possibly could. However, supporting someone who had recently been in jail was not my area of expertise. I contacted a friend of mine, sport psychologist, Simon Lloyd, who I had worked with at Collingwood for five years.

Simon was working at Fremantle at this time and though this request may have seemed slightly out of place, I knew he was the perfect person to assist me in dealing discreetly and gently with Andy. I had the greatest admiration for Simon, both professionally and as a friend. He had shown my own family such wonderful empathy and support throughout our recent adversity and I knew that he would be unbiased in describing our program and the culture of the club. I knew Simon would, like me, be glad to see such a player given another opportunity at elite-level football, but even happier to see him given another opportunity at life. Both of us could envision the hope that this story could give many others if we could help Andy to become a success story. As expected, Simon tactfully and delicately discussed the game, the club and life over lunch in a relaxed environment.

Andy was receptive to everything we discussed and appeared very focussed. You could see the glimmer of hope in him. He openly spoke about his family and the people who had supported him and stuck by him through his struggles. It was obvious that he was proud of his partner, Barbara, who was studying nursing and he also spoke lovingly of his two daughters. He said, 'This is a wonderful opportunity to help my family and set them up.' I asked him what plans he had in mind, both while playing footy and after footy had finished. He told me that his ambition was to help other Indigenous boys who were going through similar struggles. He would like to be involved in mentoring programs where he could give them hope.

Later on, when he arrived in Melbourne, I tested him and it was confirmed that he had followed the fitness program that I had set for him. Unfortunately he wasn't able to attend the altitude camp, as he was not allowed to leave the country. He was showing enormous promise and I could see him fitting into our club very well. I was pleased with his attitude and the way he had committed to the work that I had set for him, but I was more impressed with his attitude to life and how he was overcoming his setbacks and having a go. It showed me that even in the darkest times people can still possess self-belief and find that glimmer of hope. Andy had found it and grabbed it by the horns. Whether he experiences success as a player only time will tell, but what defines success for Andy is much more than his sporting achievements. It will be found in overcoming his problems and moving forward with his life.

Andy's comeback attracted some media attention. I believe Simon Overland, the Victorian Police Commissioner at the time, got it right. He said, 'I think what we're losing sight of is a fantastic story of redemption, a young man who actually has done some serious jail time and has been able to fight his way back. I'm sure he's been able to do that for lots of reasons, partly out of his own character, but partly because a lot of people stood by him. Don't give up on these people . . . it eventually will convince them that they are capable of being redeemed . . . I just prefer to focus on the fact that I think it's a wonderful story.'

Andy Krakouer—On his comeback to the AFL

I prepared myself for the worst scenario, which was going to jail. I took responsibility for what had happened and accepted the sentence. I saw Barbara, I shed a few tears. 'I'll just have to do the time given to me,' I thought.

While in jail, I asked the question, 'What am I doing here?' I had a lot of dark times. I dealt with them by thinking that others were worse off than me. I knew that I'd never take anything for granted anymore—particularly when your freedom is taken away. Being in there made me appreciate what I had in my life.

Life is good for me now. I'm doing what I love, which is playing footy and helping my family and giving them positive opportunities. I want to repay the faith back to so many people. I've got through because I controlled what I could control—that is, choosing to be around positive people and trying to approach life with a positive outlook.

Everyone, at some point in their life, will face their own setbacks or adversities. How each person responds will be unique, but one key element of coping is to build your resilience. We can be sensitive to events that may occur, but by building resistant and sturdy armour we become stronger and better equipped to face and buffer these events. This can provide us with a sense of purpose, but also, more importantly, a ray of hope.

CHAPTER 9

FORWARD THINKING

Sport is forever evolving and improving. After many world-class athletes had attempted to break the four-minute mile, in 1954 Roger Bannister was the first man to achieve this. It has since been run 17 seconds faster than this. In years to come we will see other records broken and this record of 17 seconds will seem obsolete. In the same era as Bannister, the 100-metre sprint was being run in the low-ten seconds. The Jamaican, Usain Bolt, can currently run it in 9.57 seconds. As with the mile, times for the 100-metre sprint will also improve and records will continue to be broken.

Coaches and sports scientists are continually pushing the boundaries to greater levels of athletic performance. They continue to help athletes to develop and train more vigorously to enhance their performance. At the Collingwood Football Club the focus is on developing strategies and systems to gain and sustain a competitive advantage. This can range from game strategies for combating the opposition to physiological monitoring and preparation. Coaching staff often get questioned about interventions and strategies and whether they make any difference to performance or not. They look for answers using brainstorming sessions—this environment provides the opportunity to openly question and challenge concepts and fosters innovation. Thinking outside the box often provides interesting solutions.

Interstate performance

One area where Collingwood used this technique is thinking about why AFL clubs tend to perform poorly in interstate games. This has been blamed on travel and the toll it takes on the players. At Collingwood, to try to overcome this, staff and players reflected on their successes in Melbourne and identified the positive components. Players were asked to identify what they felt influenced them in performing better in Melbourne and key personnel listened and analysed their responses.

As the season progressed, some of these responses were explored further. The club sought the input of past teams with a successful history of interstate performance, as well as personnel from other sporting codes and the opinions of experts in travel. As a result of this input and evaluation, Collingwood trialled some new interventions. Again, players were asked their opinions and a cycle of continued investigation developed. Not only did the interstate performance improve, but it was done with a healthy collaborative method that empowered everyone.

Dealing with injury

David—Nathan Buckley's hamstring

Nathan was having chronic hamstring problems early in 2005. Initially the conventional diagnosis and rehabilitation was conducted. Most hamstring injuries heal with non-surgical treatment. In general terms, a grade-one hamstring injury would see a player miss approximately three to four weeks of football. Nathan was showing signs typical of this. We had a process in place to resolve the problem and establish the effectiveness of the intervention. The alternative to surgery was physiotherapy, strengthening of the hamstring muscles and progressive conditioning, moving towards functional football training and finally, playing.

Unlike most hamstring injuries, Nathan's was taking some time to heal, which was posing a problem to all of us involved in his rehabilitation. Just when he was approaching the end of his rehab and we would think he was ready to resume to full training, the problem and pain would rise again and we would have to go back to the drawing board. We explored a myriad of investigations, including scans, MRI's, strength tests and various treatments (including alternative medicines), but to no avail.

As captain, Nathan was an integral part of the team and his leadership on the field was being missed. After the team's poor performance of 2004, the team needed him back to lead his men in 2005. His attitude and approach towards preparation and playing was outstanding. As it appeared that we were not solving the hamstring problem, it magnified the problem for Nathan, the team and us.

Nathan was 32 years old and was nearing the end of his football career. However, because of his professional attitude, his talent and his history of many accolades, we all wanted to see him play for as long as possible. We didn't believe he was quite ready for retirement and neither did Nathan. Many players at this stage of their careers become restricted by their injuries and are forced into retirement. We were not prepared to accept defeat just yet. Nathan was also determined to try everything to resume playing.

Dave Francis, Paul Blackman and I had reached a point where we had exhausted all non-invasive avenues. The MRI had shown some scar tissue, which is not uncommon, and we knew that this was typical of hamstring injuries. The club's sports physician, Paul Blackman, had assisted in surgery on hamstrings before. In our regular discussions on Nathan, he suggested that if Julian Feller, our orthopaedic surgeon, performed a minor operation to reduce the scar tissue, it might help with his recovery and help resolve the problem. We discussed the effects that surgery might have and the extra time it would take to recover. However, we also knew that we were not making any progress and felt that it needed to be considered.

Nathan was kept updated on these discussions. He had also thought we needed to explore other alternatives and agreed to surgery. We all knew, though, that there were no guarantees.

When Julian conducted the surgery, assisted by Paul, they immediately found the problem. They discovered, to their surprise, that there was one-centimetre-long tear on the surface of a tendon that attached the biceps femoris muscle, just above the knee. The surgery turned out to be a fairly simple procedure to stitch up the tear and it was completed in about half an hour.

In all the investigations that had been conducted, the rupture had been missed by scans because it was covered by scar tissue. Although surgery may have seemed like a risk at the time, if it had not been conducted we may have seen the premature retirement of Nathan. Fortunately it was successful and Nathan continued to play until the end of 2007.

Nathan's problem was not only significant for his return to playing, but it was also significant in changing how we assess scans of hamstring injuries. We now examine images from different angles to try and discover the full range of any potential problems. This whole procedure of Nathan's was time-consuming yet beneficial in not only improving our assessment of hamstrings but also allowing collaborative decision-making between player, doctors, physios, coaches and conditioning staff.

Nathan Buckley—Hamstring

I injured my knee in 2001 and I had to wear a brace for the last few rounds. I believe it was during that incident that I initially damaged my hamstring tendon. All the strength work we did on it acted as a buffer against further damage and prevented the hamstring from weakening. Unfortunately over time it weakened, which led to frustration at not being able to resolve the problem.

We were all persistent, but for every ten ideas there may be only one that works. It became a process of elimination. It got to the point where there was nothing else to do. We knew it wasn't neural so we had to go in and have a look. The procedure was unique; it wasn't common practice. Once the rupture was found and repaired, I was so relieved.

That experience taught me to never stop searching. You realise when things don't go your way that there are so many people who invest their time and effort into you and your wellbeing. I saw the frustration of the people helping me. As a professional athlete it's your responsibility to be proactive and challenge the status quo. It was comforting to know that I wasn't alone.

David Francis, Collingwood's physiotherapist—On Nathan Buckley's hamstring

We were always searching for the answer and we were looking outside the box to resolve the problem. We were passionate and keen to overcome the issue. It was a stressful period, but working as a collaborative unit and keeping to a disciplined process gave us confidence. In the culture we work in you can't afford to rest on your laurels, particularly when you think you have found the answer as there's always something else lurking around the corner. We have to be confident in our ability and remain decisive.

Avoid knee-jerk reactions

A creative work environment doesn't occur overnight—particularly in sport, when results can cause knee-jerk reactions.

It's common when teams are losing for the environment to become threatening and tenure to become unstable. When this happens, key personnel can find themselves forced to withdraw to a safe haven and become conservative, keeping to tried and proven routines and being less likely to take risks. They also become less spontaneous and imaginative and stop searching and trialling new methods. Usually the opposite is needed because the old methods are clearly not working.

When teams are being beaten, we often see unsubstantiated comments coming out and rash assumptions being made. How often do you hear after a team has lost that they are not fit? But how can this be if the week before they had a convincing win? How could a team lose their fitness in one week? What has transpired for this to occur? The answer remains pertinent to that particular club because each coach would have their individual perspective. Certainly, in days gone by, teams were given a 'flogging' on the training track after losing—almost like a punishment—and by the time they played the following week they were experiencing fatigue, which merely compounded the problem.

As with the analysis of interstate travel, it is better to see what was working over the period when they were winning. What strategies were being used that contributed to their success? Questioning is very healthy because it helps dig deeper into the problem and can provide a definitive resolution, but it must be collaborative. It must involve all those involved!

Collaborative solutions

If a coach notices that a player's work rate is dropping off in the latter part of the game, he (or the sports scientist) should ask the player if he also believes he is dropping off. If the player agrees, the questioning should continue to find out if he can suggest any reasons why. He may respond with the fact that he felt heavy going into the game and not fresh. His comments should be analysed, along with test results. If the problem can be accurately defined, a strategy can be implemented to prevent it from happening again and the problem may be solved. At Collingwood, in such circumstances, it's not uncommon that a player is given two days off from training and encouraged to spend time with his family. Back at the club staff would be investigating plausible contributing factors using evidenced-based scientific methods. If the problem was more obscure, a strategy would be developed, in conjunction with the player's input, and trialled, evaluated and re-trialled until a definitive answer is discovered.

Guy McKenna—Innovation

For me, it's all about sharing the idea, coming up with a better solution . . . that way more than one person will buy into the new direction and effort. I have no doubt that that way you'll come up with an idea that is superior and embraced by a group of people ready to buy in and make it work. At Collingwood we were constantly looking for the next advantage to stay ahead of the competition. My definition of innovation is simple: know what you've got and then turn a good situation into a better one.

Innovation through trial and error

There is never a dull moment at football clubs as they are always striving to obtain success, or at the very least, improvement. The different personalities and skills at a football club are quite diverse, but when they merge together appropriately they can form a stimulating critical mass and innovation can occur. It's not always about inventing new methods. Usually when we are solving problems we find ourselves being innovative because it is through trial and error that we find solutions. However, there's always a risk involved. In Round 11 in 2007, change was imminent and Collingwood needed a new system to stay at the top.

Mick—Interchanges

In Round 11 of 2007, Collingwood was just inside the eight, our season teetering on the edge of a disappointing fade-out. A Premiership in the near future seemed a million miles off.

The great sides of the competition that season, Geelong being the most dominant, all had A-grade midfielders who could turn a game on its head in one contest and win matches off their own boot. On closer inspection, though, they had very few, if any, B-grade players—the hard nuts who will chase all day for you and fulfil their role competently without the superstar tag. The rest of the team was made up of what I would label C-graders—efficient footballers who can go unnoticed, who will diligently complete their jobs each week. These players can lack consistency.

In comparison, the Magpies had a side of mostly B-grade footballers, developing quickly (as we know now) into efficient A-graders.

Why is this significant? Because to ever have a chance of winning a Premiership without a team full of our own A-graders, we had to find a way to neutralise the effectiveness of the opposition A-graders.

David, our midfield coach at the time, Guy McKenna, and I came up with a plan to do just that.

We looked at the game of ice hockey, where players are rotated on and off in quick succession. The players joining the action can 'explode' onto the ice for a fierce attack of less than two minutes before returning once again to the bench. This allows the team to maintain a fierce and powerful dominance on the arena for short bursts, before another group replaces them to work at the same rate. In this way, relentless pressure is kept on the opposition.

So our new plan was to increase our use of the bench, interchanging players frequently like successful ice hockey teams. Of course, with only four men on the bench at a time (excluding injury) in the AFL, we couldn't rotate more than that number each time we made a change.

From this point on, our backmen had little or no rest on the bench. Our key forwards came off once a quarter. Our high forwards (who can run further up the field and burn more energy) were to have twice-quarterly breaks. Our hardworking midfielders were to be rotated three times a quarter—never together—at an interval of two minutes off and six to seven minutes on.

We went from making an average of 44 rotations per match midway through the year to 88 interchanges a game by the end of the season.

We felt this new interchange system not only maximised the energy and efforts of our players, but limited the value of the opposition A-graders as well as smashing their C-graders. As a result, we were able to put more pressure on the ball and increase our endeavours on a tiring opposition midfield.

The proof was in the pudding when we went to Western Australia later that season to play the Eagles in a semifinal. We drew the match and had to play an extra quarter of time-on. Only the fittest of teams will prevail in this circumstance, such is the strain of a further 20 minutes of football. We won by 19 points in the end and progressed to another round of finals. West Coast kicked only two points to our three goals and three points in that time-on. Although for us it was a travelling game, our onballers still had the energy to push forward in that extra-time period.

For the preliminary final against Geelong, our number-one ruckman, Josh Fraser, had to pull out of the game the night before and we also lost Anthony Rocca during the game to an ankle injury. Replacing two big men is a difficult task at any time, but we fought bravely and whole-heartedly up to the final siren. We fell agonisingly short to lose by five points.

I still believe it was our new increased-rotation approach that got us so close to the ultimate champions, Geelong (that season they won 18 out of 22 games plus three finals, including the grand final, which they won by a record margin against Port Adelaide). We were just outclassed by a very impressive team in the end.

We continued to develop our interchange system over the following years and by 2010 we were making more than 100 changes per game. We were deemed the best in the competition at managing rotations and thus our playing list. We're convinced it contributed greatly to us winning the Premiership that season. Though the first grand final was drawn, by the start of the second grand final a week later, our players were fresh and ready to perform again. Those that were down in the first match—such as A-graders Dane Swan and Scott Pendlebury—were able to recover sufficiently because of the rotation policy and get back to their best, which was high-intensity and high-possession football.

The side-effect of our (and subsequently, other clubs') increased use of the bench led to an unprecedented rule change by the AFL. It is very rare for a governing body to make hasty changes to the rule book, but the league's hierarchy felt it necessary to do so for the 2011 season.

The research and conclusion of the AFL—that injuries increase with more rotations—vastly contradicted our own findings and evidence at Collingwood. Our soft-tissue (or fatigue) injuries had, in fact, decreased since we began rotating players more frequently. Unfortunately, a single club cannot overturn the recommendation of a ruling body and a 'sub' was introduced to our game of football.

The league bosses believed that reducing the number of available players on the bench to three and providing a substitute as a replacement player would decrease the need for and the use of rotations, concluding that fatigue and injury for the remaining players on field would therefore be reduced. They also thought it would slow the game down and keep the better players on the ground for longer, making it fairer for all. This is still contentious and has yet to be proven.

After careful consideration and planning, when the new rule came into effect in 2011, our rotations actually increased again. We experimented with the rotation policy throughout the NAB Cup series and early in the season proper, with the effect that we would still maintain high interchange numbers. Player game time was slightly elevated; the player with the least amount of game time saw an increase to above 80 per cent per game. This was done through a variety of areas, most noticeably with players spending more time in non-preferred positions (therefore developing multi-position players on the run).

Once the rules are in place, it is up to us (and all clubs) to exploit them legally as best we can for our playing group. This is how the game of Australian Rules football evolves.

Fortunately, what the club came up with had a positive result—not only did they find an effective new system, but they also developed multi-position players as a bonus. Innovation can lead to further changes by other teams as well. The level of rotations across the AFL has shown a significant increase over the last few years. Despite the AFL restricting the bench to three, with one extra player as a substitute, some clubs are achieving record numbers in their rotations.

There is never any point in dwelling on the changes that come into effect; clubs have little or no control of them. The opinion of a club is pretty irrelevant, so instead of dwelling on it, accept the change and move forward. The longer you resist it, the more you risk being left behind.

When the AFL first publicly discussed the new rule changes for the 2011 season (to a limited interchange bench or the amount of interchange rotations that could occur) Collingwood commenced discussions on various formulas and permutations to deal with it. Once the new changes had been confirmed, Collingwood was well on its way to trialling new methodologies to give them an advantage. With the pace that football moves today there was no time to lose.

Sports science and coaching can often operate in distinct silos, but the interchange story is about integrating expertise from both fields. Coaches and sports scientists must never lose sight of why they do what they do to achieve optimal sports performance. The ideal team sport environment has no room for egos pushing their own agendas; it should always be collaborative and about the team.

Knowing your role

In any team environment, people must do just that—work as a team. This is not limited to the sporting world, but exists in all environments where groups of people work together. Each person must recognise that they are an important part of this and know their role. Although this has already been recognised and discussed, what must be further examined is that everyone must know the other team members' roles. When everyone is fully aware of the other peoples' responsibilities there's little room for misunderstanding or error.

In earlier days, a football coach would control most facets of a football department. As roles became more specialised, coaches were encouraged—or sometimes forced—to make room for others with greater knowledge in specific areas. Not all coaches were able to let go of their control easily; they may have thought it showed a weakness in their leadership or looked like they were losing control. But those who could let go and delegate and encourage saw great development in their team. Instead of a lack of leadership or control, it showed great leadership.

> *Only those who will risk going too far can possibly find out how far one can go.*
>
> T.S. Eliot

Trial and error

Some concepts look great in theory but fail in practice. Like any new development or technology, testing and thorough scrutiny must be conducted to assess whether it works. Mistakes can happen because the intensity and pace of AFL football unearths so many complex intricacies. We also need to examine if we are willing to ask whether we are as good as we think we are. And are we prepared to admit it if the answer isn't positive?

Mick—When it doesn't work

No West Australian team had ever won at the Melbourne Cricket Ground when I first moved to Perth. The Eagles, as well as every senior and junior state team, had failed in every quest for victory at the home of football in Melbourne.

To win a Premiership we had to win at the MCG, so something needed to be done to shift this hoodoo. I thought I knew why winning had eluded so many West Australian teams up to this point. I was convinced it was the travel arrangements, which included a four-hour plane flight the day before a game. I also thought it was the bigger ground— the MCG's width is very different to the uniquely long Subiaco Oval. The crowd capacity at the MCG also dwarfed our own at home and introduced an intimidating factor. Finally, I'd concluded that after consistently losing, there was now a fear of failure before the game even began for every player representing a West Australian team.

So there we were in 1990, not long into my first season as coach of the Eagles, about to play Richmond at their home ground, the MCG.

My change of tactics included travelling a day earlier and completing our final training session of the week on a bigger Melbourne ground in heavier Victorian weather conditions.

We beat the Tigers by 35 points. It was a big deal in Perth; the media celebrated the fact we were the first WA team to defeat a Victorian team at the MCG. It seemed that my theories had been correct. A few adjustments to our travel and training regime was all that had been needed to get the result we wanted.

It turned out I was wrong. The following week, Round 7, we were up against a dominant Melbourne Demons team. They'd won five on the trot but were coming off a loss to Sydney upon facing us.

Again we tried our new model for travelling. We left a day earlier and trained on a big ground in wintry conditions. We were ready to win again. We lost. In fact, we were thrashed by 55 points. The entire team took a heavy knock as we were engulfed once again by the failure.

We played at home for the next two rounds and then took on North Melbourne at the MCG, only to lose again, further compounding the fact that the new formula wasn't working.

So I went back to the drawing board. We weren't scheduled to play at the MCG again that season, though we still had many games to play on the east coast and, in particular, in Victoria.

Before our clash with Carlton at Princes Park in Round 17, we decided to train at home before flying east. It wasn't a full training session, just what we called a 'touch' session at one of the larger local parks in Perth. With training out of the way we were able to make our way to Melbourne with our thoughts only on the game. We arrived the afternoon before the match, had a light stroll before a team meeting over dinner and gave the playing group the chance to have a good night's sleep. We were victorious and followed up with another win over Geelong at Kardinia Park a few weeks later.

We made the finals that year and won one game, drew another and lost two of the four matches we played at Waverley Park in Melbourne that September.

We went on to contest the finals every year for the decade I was coach of West Coast, including two Premierships played on the hallowed turf of the MCG.

We needed to try a few different factors to get the mix right. While we didn't achieve the best result for every game that we played away from home, the club did erase its fear of losing in Melbourne. I'm not sure if the Eagles still use the same travel routine that we devised in the 1990s, but I do know that playing a match in Melbourne is no longer a big issue and winning there is a common occurrence.

I remembered this process of elimination when Geelong became the dominant team of 2007. Their game plan was based on high possession, even reaching as high as the 500 mark in a match that season. Soon every club tried to follow the Cats' lead, including Collingwood. We failed miserably.

Geelong was so good at this type of game because it suited the players in the team. They had a number of terrific ball-handlers who were like football magnets, so possessing the ball in high numbers was very achievable for them. It wasn't for us.

By copying Geelong's approach we were, in fact, playing into their hands. By trying to turn our players into a replica of the Cats' team we were setting ourselves up for failure. We would always be second to the team that invented the wheel.

So once again we changed tack. We switched our plan to the application of continuous frontal pressure to try to force the high ball-handling teams (like Geelong) to turn the football over. We worked to our own strengths rather than our weaknesses, which the high-possession game plan had exposed in us.

We started to have success with this new approach and by refining our plan throughout the following seasons, with old and new players, we eventually gained ultimate success with a Premiership.

Reworking our strategies and changing our mindset once again made the difference. We were able to admit when and where we got it wrong and we worked hard until we got it right.

Alternative therapies

It's so interesting, in this world of technological advancement, that we sometimes find ourselves returning to the methods of old. For example, we no longer think that if we can't sleep, we should automatically pop a pill; people now seek massage, herbal remedies, acupuncture and yoga. Many of the natural remedies come from Eastern medicine and have ancient histories. Yet we seek them in our modern world (sometimes hesitantly) not only because of their value and credibility, but also because they often have little or no side-effects. For an athlete this is crucial to getting back on the field, as well as remaining legal in case of drug-testing.

Sleep deprivation is a common ailment among elite athletes. Because of the intensity of their role, they can find themselves under constant scrutiny. They can be affected by media opinion, comments by the less informed or by the sheer magnitude of performing in front of crowds of thousands of fans. In addition to this, they are still just people who have family, work, study, relationship and life issues.

Medication has its place; consider a player who is suffering an acute injury and requires some pain relief and perhaps surgery. Still, a number of issues can be dealt with less invasively. Relaxation techniques or meditation can provide benefits in other aspects of life, including anytime they are feeling anxious. They can develop healthy lifelong habits and continue to benefit from these techniques for the rest of their lives.

David—Meditation

After spending several minutes sitting upright in a completely relaxed but conscious state, I opened my eyes to see a very concerned coach looking at me. Mick asked me if I was all right and I told him I had been meditating.

It was 6 a.m. in our room in Flagstaff, Arizona, and I had risen early to meditate before we began our day's strenuous training program. I explained to Mick that this was something I practised regularly—twice a day, in fact. He asked why I did it and I explained that a friend of mine had taught me how to meditate after Nick had died because it had such positive benefits.

He asked me what these benefits were and I told him it slowed down your heart rate, metabolic rate and ventilation, as well as decreasing your cortisol levels, all while in a conscious state. He laughed and asked me to explain it in English. I told him that it simply relaxes you and improves your general well-being and I had noticed that I had been sleeping a lot better. He asked me if I could teach him how to do it too.

Not long after Mick had learnt how to meditate, so had a third of the players as well as several staff members. We noticed from the players' diary responses on sleep patterns and their recovery indicators that improvements were occurring. They were also commenting on improvements in their recovery. Most were initially sceptical—as I had been in the early stages—but I encouraged them to remain open-minded.

It remained everyone's personal choice; each decided whether they would try it or not. But, like me, they felt that if this method has been used for millennia, there must be some benefits to it.

Nick Maxwell—Meditation

Our lives can be full-on and the pressure to perform each week is intense. Meditation gives me the opportunity to just stop.

New methods

Any new method in sport is generally met with criticism or scepticism; when presenting an innovation one must be prepared for this. Questions arise. Is it cheating? Is it fair? Can everyone gain from its benefits? Sometimes they are fair, and sometimes they are not. And sometimes it is yet to be determined what they are. But every new trend always has its settling-in time and must go through the trials, the failures or the successes and face up to the doubters and the sceptics. It generally takes time to be accepted and adopted. Then, more often than not, it becomes a part of common practice.

David—Attracting knockers

In 2005, when we were going on our first trip to Arizona, sceptics were popping their heads up everywhere I turned. Because I had been the one pushing for the trip to train in altitude conditions, I met many people who were ready to give their opinion on how ridiculous it was. They were happy to tell me they thought it was a junket, another way of having a footy trip of the traditional kind where players partied hard with their mates, under the guise of a training camp. How far from the truth they were!

I remember being out to dinner one evening and someone I knew leaning in close to my face, sneering and telling me what a joke it was. In front of my friends, he ridiculed me and asked me how could I be so stupid as to think I had fooled people into believing that it had benefits. And costing the club so much as well! Sadly, to add to this, this person was a Collingwood supporter. Of course, these many negative opinions of altitude training were never substantiated.

Justifying its benefits was not something I needed to do to the public. I remained polite but ignored such opinions. I was so convinced of altitude training and its benefits that I was able to remain focussed and ignore public opinion. The most rewarding aspect of pushing through the negativity and doubt is that now the players believe in its benefits, train with it and endorse it to others.

It's no secret that several other AFL clubs now have altitude rooms and go on altitude camps. This can only benefit the AFL and sport in general, for now the competition is becoming greater and more even. We are seeing athletes reach great heights in their performance and we, as spectators, can enjoy wonderful displays of skill and athleticism from our footballers and sportspeople.

The AFL is working hard to become a truly national sport. Some day we may see Australian Rules football become an international sport. A sport we will look at with pride because it has originated from our own country and because some of us have played a small part in its growth.

New trends in sport are a regular occurrence and new methods are always being discovered. Most of us today are benefitting from our predecessors and their techniques. Fartlek training (running at different intensities) was developed in 1937 by Swedish coach Gösta Holmér. Using dumbbells dates back to the ancient Greeks. Yet we use both of those techniques today. Where would we be if these methods weren't shared and taught to generations of athletes years later? Where would sport be if people had not been prepared to pass on their innovations? This not only refers to techniques that worked, but also the sharing of those that failed. Although we love to see athletes perform at their best and see them raising the bar higher all the time, we don't want to see them hurt or have their careers terminated because an error occurred and others were not warned about it.

In the AFL, trends in coaching methods are becoming commonplace—the interchange rule being one example. Coaches look beyond their own football code to other sports for training or coaching methods that work well. Collingwood has utilised the relationship it has with the Melbourne Storm rugby league team. When our tackling technique needed attention, our coaches approached the Storm for tips on effective tackling.

> *Innovation is the ability to see change as an opportunity—not a threat.*
>
> Thomas Edison

New trends in recruitment

Another area where a trend is developing is in recruitment. When the national draft was first established, recruiters would look at the potential ranking of the top players and see who would fit into their club and what the club required. However, with the evenness of the draft—that is, the bottom clubs having the first selections and the more successful clubs having later ones—recruiters needed to look more closely at potential players who were further down the list. They were forced to explore whether there were other aspects of their ability and potential not initially apparent. Overnight, comprehensive physiological and psychological profiling was born.

For Collingwood, Noel Judkin, and later Derek Hine, had the foresight to see what others may not have seen. They recruited players who may not have been highly skilled as potential draftees but possessed other attributes—such as great strength or character, perseverance and determination. Our 2010 Premiership team was made up of many such players: rookies who had missed the initial draft but were later put on our rookie list, including Harry O'Brien, Alan Toovey, Brent Macaffer, Jarryd Blair, Sharrod Wellingham and Premiership captain Nick Maxwell. This trend of thinking outside the box may be something we see more often, due to the increasing limitations placed on clubs around recruiting time.

We will continue to see the AFL get faster, just as the 100-metre time will decrease. And we will continue to see coaching techniques and trends develop and improve as the game evolves. Being forward-thinking and taking risks will promote innovations. If these occur in a collaborative manner, who knows where we can go?

CHAPTER 10

PEOPLE YOU MEET ALONG THE WAY

We all know people who are always making excuses for the way they are and blaming it on other people. Sure, it's true that the people we grow up with and/or share our lives with shape us to some degree. We all meet some amazing people on our journey and yes, it can be life-altering, but we must never lose sight of the fact that we are free to make our own choices.

On the other hand, we can all remember meeting people who have left a wonderful impression. They are people whose company we enjoy and seek out. We often gravitate to these people because they have altered us in some way, usually positively. Whether it is in a brief encounter or through years of living with them, whatever your upbringing we meet certain people along the way who significantly shape and influence us.

Mick—My early influences

In my position as coach of perhaps the most famous sporting club in Australia, the Collingwood Football Club, I have been privileged to meet many people, some amazing and all with stories of their own. Indeed, this has happened at each club I was involved with in my football career. Not all of these people were sportsmen, nor were they all 'famous', but they did all have one thing in common—knowing them educated and inspired me.

Scattered through this chapter is a sample of the unusual, gifted and warm people I have been lucky enough to meet in my career and life. All of them have had a positive influence on me in their own way.

My father, Ray, never knew his father and was abandoned by his mother at birth. His grandmother raised him. At a young age his friends nicknamed him Hardy and it stuck for life. The name represented his tough and difficult upbringing. He tried to give a different life to his children, but he was struck down by the debilitating paralysis of Guillain-Barre syndrome when my sister Geraldine and I were still young. He never made a full recovery. My father taught me about persistence and courage like no other.

When I was 12 years old my grandfather, Timothy Canty, took over as my carer. He was the salt of the earth. He lived in the small Victorian country town of Gordon, which is possibly why he was so thoughtful about nature. He taught me some great life skills, the greatest one being to care for the bush. He also tried to teach me patience—which I'm still trying to come to grips with!

My wonderful mother, Marie, taught me about endurance and loyalty. In a single year she lost her mother and effectively her husband, as his health deteriorated spectacularly. She somehow continued to be a caring mother, wife and friend as she nursed my father to health. She remained one of my biggest supporters until her passing.

David—A father's influence

Every child is exposed to different influences and when I was growing up, it was sport. My dad, Ron, loved sport. This influence had come from his father and uncles. My earliest memories are of my dad telling stories about past athletes and footballers and their achievements. His knowledge and memory for facts was astounding. He could recall events and describe them in the greatest detail and we would listen to the wonderful feats some of these people achieved—sometimes being told them one time too many!

He had been an athlete himself in the early 1950s. His father, James Buttifant, had been a runner as well, but in a different form. In World War I he was an 8th Battalion signaller; his role was to take messages from one commanding officer to another because he was considered to be the fastest soldier in his battalion. I have been told these men were very brave as they were usually delivering these messages under fire from the enemy.

But my dad was not just about telling the stories and living in the past. His children were all encouraged to participate in various activities. We all competed in athletics and my brothers and I played footy as well. I have fond memories of getting up at 6 a.m. with my brothers and sister and training down at Yarra Bend in Fairfield with dad during the mid-1970s.

I remember regularly seeing a man a Fitzroy football jumper running down there. He would always say hello and give us young kids encouragement. Dad would tell us one of his stories: this man's name was Pastor Sir Doug Nicholls and he had once played football for Fitzroy and Victoria in the 1930s. Dad explained how he had done much for the Aboriginal community.

With three boys in the family we were, not surprisingly, very competitive. So when Dad set us off on our staggered starts it was on for young and old. My sister was no shrinking violet. She had to survive in a family of three brothers and she could hold her own. Perhaps that was why she became a Victorian junior 800-metre champion. As I was the youngest, Dad always ran with me and when we reached a hill he would always instruct me to look only three metres in front of me. He told me to avoid looking at the big hill ahead, just take little steps, one at a time. He reminded me to keep pumping my arms. To help me try to block out the pain he reminded me of a story he had previously told about the Ethiopian runner Abebe Bikila, who had won two Olympic marathons, one of them in bare feet. I was impressed—how could someone run that far, let alone in bare feet?

Our weekends during winter were football. I played on Saturday morning with school, Saturday afternoon with Richmond Little League, Sunday with a local team and sometimes, if I was lucky, another game if one of the teams was short. Dad was part of it all. He was president and coach of the local club and heavily involved in its operations. He was a life-long Collingwood supporter; I can still see the look on his face when I told him I was going to work for them. He was bursting with pride.

It is no surprise, therefore, that I love sport. And it's no surprise that I undertook a career in it. All these years later, with Dad no longer with us, I still think of his stories and his passion for football and athletics, and I pay tribute to his part in shaping who I am today.

Mick—Difficult moments as a leader

The first time I arrived at Victoria Park, as the newly appointed coach of Collingwood, I sat in my car for an hour before entering the clubrooms.

I can remember that hour so clearly. The emotions that were building up within me and the thoughts that were overwhelming me threatened to stop my entry into the famous stadium.

It wasn't the ground itself that froze me in my seat. I had journeyed to Victoria Park many times before, as both player and coach, and experienced both wins and losses. Nor was it the people I was to meet inside, for I knew there would be some wonderful personalities to work with at this great club. It certainly wasn't the Collingwood supporters, because rather than being intimidated by their hostility on each of my visits to the ground, I found their fierce loyalty impressive.

It was the memory of what I had left behind that was keeping me back.

Two months earlier I had left West Coast to take on this new job at the Magpies. There were many reasons for my decision to leave Perth and the Eagles, the major factor being illness among family members living in my home state of Victoria.

I had turned my back on ten years of relative success—a decade of finals and two Premierships. I had given up a winning culture. I had said goodbye to the people, many of them close mates, whose hard work and support had helped to achieve that success. It was no wonder that I still felt a very strong attachment to the West Coast Eagles.

I had accepted the job at Collingwood because they were on the bottom of the ladder. Sixteenth is sixteenth and the challenge this presented sparked a renewed passion in me. I relished the opportunity to lift the club back up to the top.

But I kept thinking about who (Rob Wiley, Trevor Nisbett, Ian Miller, Glen Jakovich, Guy McKenna, Tony Evans and Don Pyke, to name just a few) and what (football success) I was leaving behind in the west.

The thought, 'What are you doing leaving these young men?' kept plaguing me. I couldn't seem to get past the guilt of leaving behind the boys I had coached and preached to about club loyalty (as well as becoming great friends).

This was a defining moment for me. I had to break the umbilical cord that had me still attached to the West Coast Eagles.

One of things you have to do as a leader is dis-engage from emotions that can drag you down. You have to focus your energies into areas of progress to move forward. The negative thoughts and feelings don't last if you don't let them.

In one of the most difficult moments in my football career, I managed that day to put the past behind me and open the car door to a new start.

I directed all of my energy into the Collingwood Football Club. It had taken me two months to reintroduce myself to the football community, but I was ready then to do so.

I met some fantastic people at Collingwood with whom I would build a strong rapport—such as players Gavin Brown, Paul Licuria, Anthony Rocca and Nathan Buckley—while reacquainting myself with Neil Balme, a former Richmond teammate, and developing a close association with CEO Greg Swann. I surrounded myself in the coaches' box with genuine and supportive men who I trusted to come with me to the club: Dean Laidley, a player I coached at West Coast; Brad Gotch, who had a wonderful knack of coaching juniors to success; and Michael Broadbridge, also from Western Australia. And so we began to mould and implement our plan for getting the bottom team quickly into a winning mindset and back among the champion teams once again. I was over the line and wanted to bring success to this club.

I will never forget my time at West Coast, nor any other club I have been fortunate enough to play or coach at. However, while I cherish the memories, I had to cut ties to focus on finding success elsewhere.

A journey of a thousand miles begins with a single step.
Lao-tzu, Chinese philosopher

David—Learning from the master

In my mid-teens I was selected to go on a Victorian Athletics Training Camp held at Melbourne University. Many of the teenagers there had been selected because they held Victorian titles and some of us had an air of arrogance about us. Along with this, I was excited to be there and was looking forward to it, even though I didn't really know what to expect.

As the days progressed we were put into groups with various coaches. At one stage I was assigned to a man by the name of Franz Stampfl. I had seen this man on other occasions at the track when we had competed there. I remember thinking he looked a sight in his red Speedos with coconut oil-covered skin, a barrel chest and a savage crew-cut hairstyle. He was in his mid-sixties and I could sense he was a man of some importance.

I had asked Dad who 'Tarzan' was and he told me his name and that he was one of the most famous Austrian athletic coaches in track and field. He had trained the famous four-minute-miler Roger Bannister and a list of many other great Olympians, so I felt privileged to be in his group. He was slightly eccentric, but I could see he loved training athletes and he had a wealth of experience. His stance, accent and delivery all commanded respect.

I don't remember too much about the camp, but I do remember some significant events. I recall two well-known shot putters and discus throwers, Bev Francis and Gael Mulhall, demonstrating jumping and hopping exercises to increase our power. Franz used a foreign term to me at the time: he called it demonstration plyometrics. I was astounded by the power that these two women could generate and listened carefully to Franz's instruction and feedback. At one stage when I was performing he repeated frequently to me, 'If you are going to be powerful, you must train powerfully!'

The next day I was so sore from the day before! Franz was about to give us another gruelling session and he asked how I was. To avoid showing weakness I played it down and told him I was a little bit sore; Franz told me not to worry about the pain and set me off on eight 200-metre interval sprints. After the fourth one he must have noticed I was slowing down and he pulled me aside. He told me not to worry about the pain but to push through it.

Of the many training sessions I've performed over the years I still remember that day vividly. I have realised that it is not until the athlete stops and is prepared to listen, really listen, that they will gain any benefit from their coaches. When my dad was instructing me I was sometimes not listening or thought I knew better. It was not until a funny-looking man in red Speedos with a big reputation came along that I remembered all I had previously been instructed and actually took heed. After that camp there was a shift in my approach to my training and naturally my performance improved.

David—A lesson in loyalty and character

Like most kids in the 1970s, I walked to school with my brothers and sister. I was cursed with the unfortunate characteristic of prominent buck teeth, so of course I was the focus of much teasing. One day I was walking home from school with my older sister, Annemaree, and a group of older kids from another school started the usual teasing, calling me the typical names like Bugs Bunny and Bucky Beaver (names my own siblings used on me now and then). But blood is always thicker than water, as I was about to find out.

We were outnumbered and outsized, so we were hesitant and frightened. Despite this, Annemaree turned around and started sticking up for me. Most of the time she was a friendly, amicable girl, but deep down there lay a fighter. Back and forth the banter went and I was proud of my sister for sticking up for her brother three years her junior. The insults quickly shifted onto her and she got called some pretty unsavoury names.

Annemaree was not satisfied that these kids were getting her message and felt that they needed to find their manners. She threatened to take them on physically if they didn't apologise. They laughed and thought this was a joke and kept their antics up. Annemaree was far from joking and she stood up to them. She laid a punch on the biggest boy and slapped the other boy in the face. She was about to lay another punch when he turned and all the bullies ran off cowering.

When I had first seen these boys I felt small and intimidated and wanted to run away. I was wishing that my two older brothers, Paul and Mark, were with us because I was pretty worried, but they were already at secondary school. As it turned out we didn't need them. I was stunned. How proud was I of my big sister? I couldn't believe it. I was now standing ten feet tall. These big-mouthed kids shrank to miserable weaklings and had been beaten, not by my sister's fists, but by her strength and protection of her little brother.

This incident taught me my first lesson in loyalty. Annemaree, in one afternoon, on a regular trip home from school, showed me the greatest example of loyalty and character. She warned me not to mention anything to Mum and Dad or I'd cop it as well. Of course, after that demonstration I wasn't game to mention a word.

David—Professors and their belief in me

At school I was a highly energetic, inquisitive kid, but I was not the best student. I was more interested in playing football because I didn't believe I had the ability to further my education. So when I left school, I didn't have any specific ambition to do any tertiary study. My father said he didn't believe I was cut out for academia.

After working for a few years I decided that I would give uni a go, despite my dad's concerns. After some years I found myself doing my Masters in Exercise Sports Science under Professor John Carlson and Geraldine Naughton. I had found my passion, studying an area that I loved: exercise physiology. As I moved along in my study with these two tutors, I began to gain confidence and started to believe that I had some ability. One day, I remember vividly, John introduced me to one of his colleagues as his PhD student. I corrected him and said that I was doing a Masters. He rebutted me and said, 'No, you will be converting from your Masters to a PhD.'

I was floored. I realised that this man believed that I was capable of completing study at the highest level. I was thrilled to think that this was how he and Geraldine viewed me. I had a small chuckle, thinking back to school when I was in Year 8 and the teacher had said to me, 'You're an idiot, Buttifant! What are you?' and proceeded to make me repeat it several times. How fortunate it was that these two mentors had entered my life. They nurtured my passion and taught me to become independent in my learning. I learnt the value of planning and developed the research skills that I still continually use. Little did they know the effect that this positive remark had on me. I am indebted to them because they opened up a new world for me.

As my career in sport has unfolded I have had the benefit of meeting many other influential professors. At Collingwood we run a sports-science forum where we have several experts gather and present different theories, concepts and research. One professor I have had the privilege of working with is Allan Hahn from the Australian Institute of Sport. His knowledge and experience in exercise sports science is well renowned and highly respected. Allan, John and Geraldine have inspired me with their expertise and the way each of them have become experts in their fields. None of them aspired to receive accolades or notoriety and yet each deserves them in spades. I have the greatest admiration for their modest, unassuming way of becoming leaders in their fields. They taught me that everyone can learn. They also taught me the value of nurturing and mentoring.

David—Confirming my philosophies

In 1999, while I was working at Homebush, Olympic Park in Sydney, I was involved in an athletics workshop of about 10 to 12 middle-distance coaches. Two Australian track-and-field Olympic gold medallists, Herb Elliott and Ralph Doubell, were presenting their theories and philosophies on middle-distance training.

It was interesting to hear their theories. Franz Stampfl had coached Ralph Doubell and the eccentric Percy Cerutty had coached Herb Elliott. Herb had won the 1500-metres gold medal in Rome in 1960 and Ralph had been the last Australian male to take Olympic gold at the track when he won the 800-metre event in Mexico City in 1968.

Ralph's strong views had a lot of merit and he was extremely interesting to listen to. He reflected Franz's scientific methods. When Ralph spoke he did not hold back on giving his strong opinions. He said that for Australia as a country to be successful we had to train a lot harder and with greater intensity, even at the risk of injury.

Herb Elliott supported a lot of Ralph's principles of training and performance. But he also spoke philosophically about life and sport. He reflected many of Percy's ideals. He discussed quality versus quantity in training and how too much can actually compromise your performance. As a young sports scientist, it was so confirming to hear his philosophies. He spoke about character, the people you should surround yourself with, knowing yourself and taking responsibility. He also spoke about passion, hard work, pushing the boundaries, competing against yourself and remaining honest, particularly with yourself.

He went on to discuss life's challenges and one of his comments resonates with me still: 'Obstacles in life are gifts from God.' Instead of shying away from adversity we should meet it and learn from it to become better and allow it to enrich our lives. Everything he said reflected all the principles that I believed in. I could actually see the connection between sport and life. All my years of study had provided me with the theory and knowledge, but it wasn't until I heard one man's story in that 30 minutes that I realised that I had already formed my own philosophies and here he was confirming them. I felt like I had had a revelation and my vocation was clear.

Mick—Wayne Walsh

One of the smartest football minds I have ever come across belonged to a man by the name of Wayne Walsh. Wayne was a South Melbourne and Richmond footballer and it was at the latter club that I first met him.

Wayne was older and more entrenched in the squad than I was so our paths didn't initially cross too often except to wear the same yellow and black jumper each Saturday (the only day on which VFL games were played back then).

When I took the coaching job at Footscray at the end of 1983, Wayne, as chairman of selectors, was one of the first men to welcome me to the club.

Knowing the extent of his football knowledge and eager to find out what he could pass on from his tutelage under the great Norm Smith (a six-time Premiership coach with Melbourne in a dominant era), I was keen to have Wayne involved with the team and coaching staff as much as possible.

His brash manner didn't help him as a coach himself (at amateur level), nor did it endear him to the squad, so his day-to-day association with the players was limited and, at times, strained. However, it was his first-class comprehension of the game that gave me the opportunity to improve my own approach—a vital support for a young and inexperienced coach. In my eyes, he had an unbelievable insight into modern-day coaching and was perhaps years ahead of his time in his thinking.

Mick—Sir Alex Ferguson and Sir Bobby Robson

Whether you're a Premier League soccer fan or not, most people have heard of Sir Alex Ferguson. He is the most successful football manager in British history with almost 50 trophies won, over 30 of them with Manchester United. He has been at the helm at Old Trafford since 1986.

I have had several short meetings with Sir Alex and the thing that stood out most to me each time was the way he naturally commanded respect. I was lucky to be in the Man U rooms after a victory once. I could immediately see why he is dubbed 'The Boss', with the likes of David Beckham and Ryan Giggs looking up to him as their leader. I could see that they played to please him. I was impressed, encouraged and inspired by this man of accomplishment.

This is not a person who does things in half-measures. He is ruthless and can be harsh. When

I asked him how he maintains the urgency of the group after reaching the pinnacle of Premier League soccer on so many occasions, he answered, 'When a player reaches 30, if he hasn't won a title by then he's not going to win one at 31, so I trade him or sell him.' Simple as that. (However, since then he has kept Giggs and sold Beckham—but not before he helped win titles.) He was horrified to hear of our AFL draft system where league rules and club dealings override the influence of money.

Meeting Sir Bobby Robson, English soccer player and manager, was an entirely different experience altogether.

I witnessed his coaching style in his declining years at Newcastle, in northern England. His philosophy was in stark contrast to the Manchester United manager. When his team won, up-to-date scientific formulas went out the window. The players were allowed to drink to the victory and delay their recovery work until the following day or later. When they lost they were punished with an old-fashioned flogging on the pitch and a witch-hunt.

It showed me then that this manager relied heavily on the past (and his own long-ago experiences in the game) and hadn't adjusted to the present.

In comparison, Alex Ferguson had a much finer edge. The Manchester United coach utilised all available current research, strategies, equipment and facilities to give his players and the club every chance of success.

Needless to say, Bobby Robson's Newcastle team failed more often than it succeeded—not only on the pitch but also off it—by failing to progress as a club. His science and conditioning staff were left disillusioned each time the procedures they put forward weren't adhered to.

Did I learn much from European soccer? No. Did I learn from the people involved? Yes—particularly from watching and meeting the definitive coach, Sir Alex Ferguson.

Mick—John Kennedy

The legendary coach of Hawthorn and North Melbourne, John Kennedy, is a marvel. As a young coach I was in awe of him. I was always on the lookout for an opportunity to sound him out about coaching, but I quickly realised I had to earn my stripes before he would even acknowledge my existence.

That acknowledgement came in 1985. Footscray met North Melbourne in a semifinal, the winner to progress to the preliminary final. We won, 137 to 107, which meant John Kennedy's Kangaroos were out of the finals race.

I happened to meet John in the car park after the match as we made our way to our cars. It was a very brief meeting in which he went out of his way to congratulate me; I expressed my thanks and commiserated with him. It meant so much to me. With those few words of congratulation he gave me an indication of the right and wrong way of coaching. To me it was acknowledgment that I was doing okay.

David—Footy mates bring hope

All sportspeople make great friends along the way playing whatever it is they play. As we mature and move from one team to another we meet a large number of people whose company we enjoy and within these groups we forge some wonderful friendships.

For me the sport was football and the team was Box Hill in the then VFA, where I was playing under past AFL player Peter Francis. Peter and I had played together at Richmond. I came to Box Hill when our eldest child, Nick, was a baby and I played there for several years. It was a good club to be at both football-wise and socially, as many other players at the club had young families too. Interestingly enough, the friends that I have remained in closest contact with from there were single at the time. In fact, they were a bit younger than me but we all shared similar ideals and values. As the years have gone by they have become family men themselves so we have all the more in common.

Not long after Nick died, Jarrod O'Neill, Darren Brusnahan and I gathered together for one of our early-morning breakfasts. We were discussing his death, our other children, parenting and life in general. Our conversation started to head towards how challenging life can be for kids and how parenting is all the more difficult when you are trying to help them. We discussed how we felt that there was not a lot out there, if anything, to help parents when their teenagers are struggling.

We decided to form a foundation that would help parents and their teenagers to build relationships. That morning the N.I.C.K. Foundation was born. We felt that with our experience and skills we could establish some type of group where people could share their stories of struggles and how they got through them. We also felt that these people did not need to be experts in any area to understand the problems, they just needed to have experienced them. If they shared their experiences with others it would help people to not feel so alone, knowing others had been through similar times.

The foundation is still new and finding its feet, but it is growing and we are continuing to receive support from many people. Some high-profile people have given generously of their time to help us by sharing their stories with others.

As I think back I feel so very fortunate to have met so many wonderful people through sport. Who would have guessed all those years ago, when I started playing for Box Hill and this blond, blue-eyed little boy was running wildly around the football change rooms, that some time down the track we would have formed a foundation named in his honour? Who would also have guessed the support this foundation would gain with the many family and friends who have already poured many hours of their time to help us in our pursuit? I left that early-morning breakfast some time back full of hope and counted my blessings for the wonderful people I have in my life.

Mick—Peter Simunovich

Peter Simunovich is an award-winning football journalist who was *The Sun's* sports editor when I met him. He now lives in New York and writes freelance for various publications, including *The New York Times*.

As soon as I met him I knew he could be trusted and that I wouldn't get burnt by him. This was very important as a young player and coach, as journalists seem increasingly intent on making a name for themselves with front-page football headlines. In the early 1980s, there were around 50 AFL-accredited journalists. Now there are well over 1000 journalists reporting on Australian football. Suffice to say that in this dog-eat-dog world, a headline is gold.

Peter, for all of the stories he 'broke' in AFL, remained true to his profession and loyal to his friends. He is an absolute gentleman.

Since his move overseas, we have remained in contact. On one trip to New York several years ago, he managed to set up a visit into the inner sanctum of the New York Jets for Nanette and myself. It was brilliant, informative and an eye-opener—particularly regarding player safety and welfare away from the club environment. With large salaries and lots of free time players become susceptible to drugs, betting and other unlawful activities.

Peter no longer writes about AFL, instead focussing on the unusual for his features. He has written on everything from the New York Mafia to the down-and-out living on the streets of New York. His stories are perceptive and sensitive and I find them totally inspirational.

I still use Peter as a sounding board for moments when I am on display in the fish bowl of the AFL environment—difficult times, celebrations and even for this book. His words of wisdom are invaluable.

Mick—Alan Schwab

I met the late Alan Schwab before he became a VFL administrator, when he was still secretary of the

Richmond Football Club. He was known as a wonderful clubman. He came from an era when you won at all costs and by any means. The Tigers had a run of good fortune in his years there, with three Premierships from four grand finals.

He understood football, the game, the clubs and the players. He worked diligently for many years to get the AFL, as an organisation and competition, performing at its best. He knew what the clubs needed to function at their optimum and he put the players and their needs back at the top of the agenda.

Perhaps his most prolific work, though, was in helping transform the Victorian Football League into the Australian Football League.

After I took the West Coast coaching job I found out that Alan had highly recommended me for the position and for that I was very grateful.

I guess, in a way, the 1992 Premiership with the Eagles became my thankyou to him. It was the first time the cup had been taken away from Victoria. In the rooms after the match I saw Alan and Ross Oakley (another AFL administrator involved in the national setup) and I could see that this was their moment of glory. Their foresight in creating a truly national football competition had finally been validated. Alan's hard work and loyalty to the game had paid off and I was especially pleased for him.

I was as shocked as anyone by the news of his passing the following year. He had been living in Sydney at the time, trying to help resurrect the Swans. The club was in dire straits both on and off the field and, as usual, Alan wanted to play a part in getting Sydney back on its feet. He died in the prime of his life. He was loved by so many in the football environment and for that I'm sure his family receives some comfort.

Mick—Denny Schwartz

Sponsors come and go in football, depending on the times, money and the opportunity to market and sell their product. However, I remember one particular sponsor of Footscray because of the man in charge.

Footscray desperately needed sponsors because of the financial strain it was under. Actually finding sponsors willing to pour big money into a club from the western suburbs with only a 1954 Premiership to its name was another story.

East Coast Jeans became a major sponsor of the club in the early '80s, but more than that, as head of the company, Denny Schwartz became a major supporter of the people within the club. He was a great friend and mentor to many of the players, always prepared to help out in times of struggle.

He showed me that some people are just willing to go that extra mile for others, asking nothing in return. He was a man of means, a good sponsor with money to give to the club. But he also made it a partnership, providing business skills, knowledge and support.

He eventually sold the business but stayed loyal to me. We had built a close bond at the Bulldogs and when I left for West Coast, he followed as a supporter and then also to Collingwood.

One year, on a trip to the United States, he introduced me to a man by the name of Jack Faulkner. He was an American football administrator, a forward scout and in recruitment for the LA Rams (now St Louis). An elderly gentleman, he had coached the Denver Broncos in the time of the great Vince Lombardi.

He was so good at his role and so committed to the organisation that when the LA Rams moved to St Louis, Jack, at the age of 66, was asked to continue his job (with a ten-year contract on offer).

When he, Denny and I had a long conversation, he impressed on me the utter importance of opposition analysis as well as the importance of tracking players from a young age (early teens) before deciding to recruit them.

After hearing his words of wisdom and experience, I decided to run a training camp for rookies at Footscray so that we could have a closer look at the football talent on offer ahead of the national draft. This was eventually taken over by the AFL and is run annually for all clubs at the Australian Institute of Sport in Canberra.

David—Learning in unlikely places

The life of a scientist is full of research, exploring theories and sharing them with others. One aspect of this is attending and presenting at football, sports-science and medicine conferences. This is always difficult for me because many of these conferences are on during the football season and flying overseas can be a tight squeeze.

In May last year I was returning home from one such trip where I had presented at a conference in Orlando, Florida. When checking in for our flight from Los Angeles I was delighted to be upgraded to business class. I had been away for five days with a short, but busy, schedule squeezed in between two weekends of football so the idea of being able to sleep on the last leg home was something I was very much looking forward to.

As I was boarding the plane I gave a nod of hello to a couple in business class who I guessed to be in their mid-sixties. I was taken aback by how unwell I thought the husband looked. But I kept moving, settled into my seat and was soon asleep. I was later woken by movement next to me and sat up to notice the lady I had seen earlier trying to rouse her husband from sleep. She appeared to be quite agitated and I offered my assistance. As I got up to help, I immediately knew that her husband was dead. Although I went through the correct proced-ures to check more accurately for this, I knew I was right and that it was too late to use a defibrillator to resuscitate him. I had seen death first-hand very recently and I knew this man had passed away.

I quietly turned to the lady, who was looking worriedly at me, and knew I had to tell her the truth. I explained that I was very sorry to tell her the news but her husband had passed away. She questioned me and asked me to check again. I reassured her that I would call someone to help, but I knew the truth needed to be told. I notified the flight attend-ants and shortly after a doctor was paged, but he only confirmed what I had said.

The staff handled everything very discreetly. The other passengers were unaware of what had tran-spired and were either asleep or resting. I could only imagine her pain. To lose your partner while so far from home, family and friends, high up in the air with no way of communicating with them, must have been terrible. When we had lost Nicholas, our comfort had been calling people who came to our immediate aid. This left me with one thought: I had to be those people for this lady. There was nothing else I could do. I settled down next to her and did my best to reassure her. I asked her name, her husband's name and about where they had been. I inquired where they had lived and about her family and their life.

I learnt much about her and what a brave woman she was. They had been on a holiday to the US. They had downsized their farm in country Victoria and had decided to go away. Her husband had been unwell while they were away and had been in hospital. They decided to cut their trip short and come back home. Unfortunately, they had not made it in time for him. While we were talking, the pilots had notified ground staff in Melbourne and her family was on their way to meet her.

I don't know how long I had slept on that flight or how long we talked. I only know that it is usually a 15-hour flight from Los Angeles to Melbourne and somewhere in the middle of that, a lady sitting near me had lost her husband. I knew that my upgrade to business class next to this woman was meant to be. I had seen and felt the harsh experience of death first-hand and could completely empathise with what she was going through, but on a different level. I explained to her that I had not lost a partner, but I had lost my father and a son in the last few years and I could, in some way, understand what she was going through.

When we landed the plane was held up as the federal and local police boarded and went about their business in a very sterile manner. The remaining passengers had become aware of what had happened and were all fussing. There was much anxiety and confusion; I wanted to remain with the woman but I was moved out of the way. I had spent hours with her and had learnt about her life and experienced her suffering. Here were people doing their job, but showing little or no empathy towards her or her situation.

I insisted on being allowed to say goodbye to her. I gave her a hug and wished her all the best. I had already given her my name but was aware that in the confusion she may not remember it. I walked through customs and messaged my wife. As I went through my phone I found a message telling me that a friend of ours had just passed away. It was with relief that I saw our car pull up because I suddenly realised how exhausted and mentally drained I was. I got in and started weeping, much to Maria's concern.

As we discussed what had happened I realised how ironic life is. I had gone to a conference to share knowledge as well as receive it, yet my greatest learning experience of that whole trip happened on the way home on an aeroplane.

Mick—Rudy Webster

Rudy Webster was a trained radiologist who became a counsellor in the late 1970s. He was also a very handy cricketer and played county cricket in England while studying. He worked with the world-dominating West Indian cricket team; big names he counselled included the likes of Viv Richards, Clive Lloyd, Michael Holding and Joel Garner.

While living in Melbourne with his wife Lindy, he also became involved with the Richmond Football Club. In 1979, I was very glad that he did.

Early in the 1979 season, I severely injured my leg, requiring a full ankle reconstruction and partial knee reconstruction. The surgeon informed me that this would take a fair amount of time to recover from; time that I did not have.

For perhaps the first time in my career I was finding it tough to firstly regain confidence in my body and secondly to physically get myself back. The Tigers' selectors wouldn't consider me until I did so.

With his very balanced view of life, Rudy took me under his wing. He got me thinking about what was in front of me, not what was behind me. He had me change from a negative mindset to a positive one.

I returned to the track with renewed energy. I played all but two games (due to suspension) of the 1980 season, including the grand final and Premiership. I owe that to Rudy—I have no doubt that I would have struggled to return to playing at all had I not received his guidance.

We became friends after that and so did our wives. It has been a while, though, since we've been in contact as Rudy now lives in the Caribbean (his home is in Barbados). He is still actively involved in sport and medicine and I'm sure he is still helping people.

David—Those that make you laugh

In a sport like ours the pressure can be enormous. In the heat of the game, instructions are hurled from the coach's box via the phones to the interchange bench and colourful invective is common. You need a thick skin; these comments are never really personal. It helps to keep a sense of humour. It's not uncommon to get comments from Walshy in the coaches' box—impatient for an injury update from the bench—like, 'Do I have to wait to read it in the *Herald Sun* tomorrow?'

When I first started at Collingwood there was this energetic upbeat bloke who reminded me of one of those friendly Staffordshire bull terriers. He was known to everyone as Maxi. I liked Maxi from the beginning because we often shared many laughs together and I was attracted to his sense of humour. His role on game day was to take instructions from Mick and pass them on to the bench.

One time we were playing at the MCG and it was the debut for young player Tristen Walker. By halfway through the third quarter he was cramping and was signalling to the bench to come off. It was a hard first game playing on Matthew Richardson, the power-running Richmond forward, who had been playing very well. I alerted the coaches' box that he needed to come off because he was cramping. Mick yelled into the phone, 'Well let's go and tell the umpires to stop the game because one of our players is cramping!' Maxi and I smirked at each other and ignored Tristen's pleas to come off.

At three-quarter time we were approaching the huddle and Maxi nudged me, grinning, and said, 'Hey

Butters, get over to those umpires and tell them to call off the game.' I laughed to myself and I still have a smile when I report the message to the coaches' box today that one of our players is cramping and I think back to that particular game. It highlights to me how, even in the heat of the battle, a little chuckle can keep your sanity.

The locker-room mentality in footy clubs among the players and staff is full of funny incidents. Often these remain within the group, but there was another event with Maxi that still brings a smile to my face. At the end of the 2002 season, I was called upon at the last moment to chaperone a footy trip to Cancun, Mexico.

On our first evening, I managed to get all the boys home after a good night out. Back in the room I was sharing with Maxi, as I walked to bed in the dark, trying not to wake him, I slipped on the tiled floor. I 'faced-planted' the bedside table and blacked out for a second. When I came to I saw stars and crawled into bed. I was totally exhausted from the travel and thought I was sweating from the Mexican heat. In the darkness I tried to wipe the sweat from my face.

I awoke in the morning to hear Maxi saying, 'What did you get up to last night? Did you get into a bit of strife?' I asked what he was on about and further thanked him for bailing out on me last night. He told me he had brought a group home earlier, but was insistent about what I had got up to, telling me I was covered with blood. It was all over my face and my bed. I went into the bathroom and realised that it wasn't sweat I'd been wiping from my face the night before but blood. The irony of it all was that I was there to make sure everyone got home safely and yet I was the one who had ended up having a mishap. Maxi gave me grief and told everyone I had rolled in drunk after being punched up by some small Mexicans. Burnsy jibed that I wasn't setting much of an example as a chaperone.

Later, while I was lying by the pool recovering, Burnsy offered me some sunscreen. When I looked in the mirror later I worked out why he'd been snickering—he'd given me fake tan! I looked like I'd spent too many hours in the solarium.

For every serious moment in sport there are as many funny ones. I thank all the guys who have given me a laugh and still do along the way, because it can take the heat off, especially during high-pressure times.

Mick—Peter Sidwell

The man who would ultimately become one of my closest mates and business manager, Peter Sidwell, was appointed vice president of the Western Bulldogs when I arrived there in 1984.

His business acumen and direct approach, as well as his sense of humour and likeable character, made him a stand-out in his position with the club. It's no coincidence that he has always been extremely successful in his own corporate ventures; recently he developed and launched the Melbourne Heart Football Club in the soccer A-League.

He has become a close confidant to me, someone who I trust completely. Even though he began as an Essendon supporter and was on the board at the Bulldogs, he stayed loyal to me as I moved from club to club. We have helped one another through difficult times in both our personal and professional lives over the years.

As a manager, he always has my best interests at heart. His business and financial advice is invaluable.

Mick—Steven Ray

Steven Ray was playing half-forward for the Saints when I joined the squad. We became mates straight away and our friendship survived a true test when I replaced him on the bench in the 1972 finals series for St Kilda. Two years after first meeting, he was best man at my wedding.

Steven is a football contradiction—not that I like to stereotype footballers. He was a superbly gifted footballer in his early life and a piano tuner later. He excelled in one and is still excelling in the latter.

I have an album full of West Coast Eagles Premiership photos thanks to Steven, after he talked his way onto the field after the 1992 Grand Final to capture the celebrations on camera for my family and myself. That sums up the man that he is. We can go months without speaking and then when we catch up it's as if we talk every day. From Steven I have learnt humility and loyalty.

Mick—Developing relationships

One of the things you must do as a coach or a leader is to get to know your staff or team on a more personal level. I don't mean you have to befriend everyone, I simply mean to find out who the individual is and what makes them tick. In any workplace, there's a common objective, so it's imperative to form a bond with the people striving for the same goal as you. It will be a different relationship to that with family or friends, but it will be an important union in achieving success. Many of the associations you make most probably won't develop beyond the workplace, but in some cases they will.

Looking back on my time in football I am lucky to have formed some true friendships and close bonds with people I may otherwise never have met.

Shane O'Sullivan currently sits on the bench at Carlton. I first met him in 1978 when we were both part of the Richmond squad. Shane unfortunately didn't make the cut, so I didn't meet him again until I took on the coaching role at Footscray, where he was general manager. Though I remembered him from Punt Road, his memories were of me as a more experienced player taking him under my wing and trying my best to help him through his short time at the Tigers. I had always aimed to do this with new and developing teammates, but I was surprised and pleased it had left such an impression on him.

We worked closely and diligently in our years together at the Bulldogs and it was ironic that this time it was Shane helping me in my early days as a young, inexperienced coach.

Over the next 20 years I always received a phone call or text from Shane before the start of each football season and, although working for the opposition, we talked as often as we could.

Steven Nash was the football manager when I first arrived at the Footscray Football Club's Whitten

Oval, and we had an instant rapport. Steven and I clicked as a working duo and provided support for each other as leaders at the club. My wife, Nanette, and Steven's wife (then girlfriend), Janet, formed a close friendship too. We were often visitors in each other's homes and, after the arrival of the two Nash boys, our children spent many hours playing together.

When I left Footscray for the West Coast Eagles, Steven followed. I respected his reluctance to uproot his family and move to Western Australia (as we were doing) and I was able to secure him a position with the club in his home city of Melbourne as the east coast manager of the Eagles. This lasted for the whole ten years that I was coaching there (and beyond).

When I moved to Collingwood, Steven stayed with West Coast so working at separate clubs therefore had a naturally negative effect on our alliance.

My bonds with both Shane and Steven were built through hard times at the Western Bulldogs. We worked from old clubrooms with a lack of funds to address any problems. The Western suburbs held a stigma that made it difficult to sell memberships beyond the diehard supporters. On the field we had ups and downs with a promising list that still needed time to develop. Perhaps it was this hardship that strengthened our connections.

Earlier in my football career I met Robby Wiley, a multiple best-and-fairest winner from the West Australian Football League club who was recruited by Richmond in 1979. Our bond was created through a forced stint on the sidelines. We were both injured

that year and obliged to endure weeks of rehabilitation. The shared hard work and frustration of
recovery reinforced our link as we got to know each
other's football strengths and weaknesses as well
as each other's identities away from the game.

Perhaps it was our joint love of a prank and a
good joke, or perhaps it was just timing, but we
quickly became the best of mates. So too our wives,
as Nanette formed a strong friendship with Marcia, helping her to adjust to life in Melbourne. Their
three girls are of similar ages to our two boys, so
once again our children extended our connection.

What ultimately bonded us forever was the 1980
Premiership that we both played in for the Tigers.
Sharing such success forms a connection for the
members of a team like no other. This was our first
taste of football glory; the second and third came
with West Coast in 1992 and 1994. While I was the
coach, Robby was my sidekick—the team runner and
informal selector. I relied heavily on his support and
advice in those years together at the Eagles. Robby
remained in Perth when we moved back to Melbourne and Collingwood and tragically lost Marcia
to cancer in 2005. Robby has moved to Melbourne
since and our friendship has once again flourished,
taking on a new dynamic with the changes in our
lives.

In 2010, I invited Robby to spend a week at
Collingwood to observe the players, staff and general
environment of the club. His advice and recommendations at the end of that time were invaluable and
I took them all on board to make changes for the
better. He is someone who I can trust to always be

honest and reliable. Our friendship has endured many years of football, loss, success and life, and I am a better person for it.

Trevor Nisbett was the football manager at West Coast when I took the reins there. He is now the chief executive officer of the club. A long and successful stint working closely, day to day, forged a lifelong connection. We regularly catch up when in the same state and wished each other well for every football season, knowing the tough and turbulent winter ahead we would each face.

Bill Sutherland was the head trainer at the Eagles for the entire decade I was in Perth. Not only was he a remarkable and efficient trainer for the players and myself, but also his wonderful and caring demeanour made him (and his wife, Rhonda) the perfect substitute grandparents for our four children who were missing their extended family. Nanette and I are so grateful for their contribution to our life in the West and our friendship with them continues today.

There are so many others I could list here: Stephen Wallis, Doug Hawkins, Guy McKenna and Glen Jakovich, to name a few.

I wouldn't say that I have come away from my life in football with a multitude of best mates, but friends, yes. I remember a conversation I had with Paul Licuria once when I asked him how many best mates he had. He replied that he had many. I said, 'No you don't, they are just acquaintances. Your true friends will be lifelong mates and of those there will be few.' He refused to believe me until his playing career ended and he came to me, upset. He had realised that this was the unfortunate truth. He had many colleagues and acquaintances, but very few genuine friends. I asked him again how many people he would label as a friend in his life and he said, 'Two, maybe three.'

'That puts you ahead of most—you are doing well,' I replied.

Most people we cross paths with in life are there for a reason. They are important to us at the time and we each take from the other what we need before moving on. This is so often the case in a team or business scenario.

Our life's journey takes us on many courses, each one leading in a different direction. We won't all tread the same road. This is why so many of the people we meet move on and become someone who we once knew. Our true friends may also take an alternative route, but they will meet us at any waypoint at any time and we will do the same for them. They may be few and far between, but the real friends we welcome in life are worth all the sacrifices we make along the way.

Mick and David have shared many stories here about their journey. The Mick Malthouse–David Buttifant partnership is only one aspect of their lives—of who they are. It was circumstance or fate that led them both to choose sport as their careers and share ten or more years working together, but it is their passion that has led them to find their vocations.

Working in the sporting world is like riding a rollercoaster of wins and losses, people coming and going and the game itself is forever changing. The constant is the values that sport is built upon—we are all connected, from the fan to the superstar. Sport engenders values that have been there since its inception. It builds character. It brings people together and encourages values such as commitment, perseverance and resilience. It teaches us to be patient and selfless and to help others to become better—nurturing qualities like tolerance and self-belief.

These stories have ranged from triumph to tragedy and some may make you laugh or cry. Whatever the effect, it is through these stories that Mick and David provide a glimpse of who they are and the experiences that have made them so. There will be many more on life's path and everyone will be tested many times, for life is a journey and you seldom know what lies around the next corner. But you can be sure that somewhere in these experiences, you will find yourself at times toiling like the ox, and at other times patiently waiting like the earth.

ACKNOWLEDGEMENTS

We would like to acknowledge the hard work and support of the following people:

Christi Malthouse—who gave so much insight and assistance with Michael's writing.

Stuart Neal—thank you for your honest feedback and for helping the vision become possible.

To all the present and past players, coaches and football staff who have contributed in some way to this book—thank you for allowing us to share your stories.